The Philosophical Golfer

Volume I: From Ancient Greece through the Middle Ages

Dr. Andrew Sola

PGA Professional Bruce Loome

Copyright © 2014 Andrew Sola and Bruce Loome

The right of Andrew Sola and Bruce Loome to be identified as the authors of this work has been asserted by them in accordance with sections 77 and 78 of the Copyright, Designs and Patents Act 1988.

All rights reserved. No part of this book may be reprinted or reproduced or utilized in any form or by an electronic, mechanical, or other means, now known or hereafter invented, including photocopying and recording, or in any information storage or retrieval system, without permission in writing from the authors. For further information, contact andrewsola1@hotmail.com.

Cover Design by Hauke Hatzelhoffer

ISBN-13: 978-1505644623
ISBN-10: 1505644623

For Bob and Deb

and

For Arthur

CONTENTS

	Acknowledgments	vii
	Introduction	ix
1	The Pre-Socratic Golfer	1
2	The Socratic Golfer	15
3	The Platonic Golfer	33
4	The Aristotelian Golfer	48
5	The Cynical Golfer	59
6	The Hedonistic Golfer	68
7	The Epicurean Golfer	79
8	The Stoic Golfer	89
9	The Theological Golfer	106
	Conclusion	135

ACKNOWLEDGMENTS

Andrew would like to thank the innumerable people who have helped with this book, including Bruce, Mom, Dad, Anna, Jono, Gary, and Hauke. Last but not least, he would like to thank all of his past, present, and future teachers and students. Their thirst for knowledge is a constant inspiration.

Bruce would like to thank the many people who have helped him grow as a teacher and player over many years and who have enabled the writing of this book. Special thanks must go to Andy for his academic expertise and continual help with the book, and also my special thanks to fellow professionals Tiger Woods and Justin Rose for the many insights and personal moments I have been privileged to share with them over the last fifteen years.

INTRODUCTION

The Origins of Sport and Thought

Andrew Sola

SPORT and thought, physical exertion and mental labor, golf and philosophy—these activities have always been fundamentally connected. They define our humanity in the most basic way, and the one is inseparable from the other.

Nevertheless, we modern couch potatoes often forget that early thinkers insisted on the necessary connection between a healthy body and a healthy mind. In the ancient world, sports and education were much more closely linked than they are today. When creating his ideal state in the Republic (circa 5th century BC), the ancient Greek philosopher Plato insisted that the state should put equal emphasis on creating the appropriate philosophical and physical attributes in its children. Plato believed that exclusive training in one or the other caused serious character defects. The person wholly devoted to sport "becomes an unintelligent philistine, with no use for reasoned discussion and an animal addiction to settle everything with brute force. His life is one of clumsy ignorance, unrelieved by grace or beauty." On the other hand, the person devoted only to philosophy becomes spiritless, "his energy degenerates into peevishness and ill temper and he is subject to constant irritability."

Plato insists that physical and mental training must be combined. When they are, sport develops the virtues of courage, confidence and self-control, and philosophy develops the traits of gentleness, moderation and wisdom. All golfers should recognize that both sets of virtues are essential to playing golf well.

Plato's understanding of the connection between the mind and body follows us in the development of the language we speak as well: the Greeks exercised in the nude, and the Greek word *gumnos* means nude; *gumnasion* is, in English, our school gymnasium—the room in which education and sport are explicitly joined. In short, sports and thought have been inextricably intertwined throughout human history.

Although an early philosopher like Plato established this connection as far back as the 5th century BC, the origins of sport and thought reach further back into prerecorded history. Indeed, I would suggest that philosophy was born in the same way that sport was—with the emergence of organized and stable human societies.

If we imagine a pre-civilized world, it is difficult to see how we would have had time either to think or to play golf. Indeed, we would have lived a difficult life, worried about saber-toothed tigers clawing us to bits and wooly mammoths goring us with their tusks, not to mention enemy tribes clubbing us to death and stealing our women and children. Golf certainly would have been a difficult pastime. Our ancestors' minds were occupied with the basics: food, water, clothing, shelter, and safety.

However, these cave dwellers probably played games as they learned the fundamentals of recreation. Things resembling balls were probably used—round stones or rolled twine might have worked. They could be rolled, kicked or thrown at targets on the cave floor. Indeed, balls seem to exist in all cultures, as do ball games. The golf ball is therefore a direct link to our primal history.

A good club would have come in handy for our ancestors as well—our hands with their opposable thumbs are perfect for grasping sticks. Indeed, we have a natural affection for the golf club because of its primal use. Every time we walk a golf course, club in hand, we are repeating what our oldest ancestors did in the plains and forests thousands and thousands of years ago. When we search for our sliced drives in the trees, we are reenacting some of the most primitive and natural of human activities: we are the lone hunter, searching for a small mammal to bludgeon and carry home for dinner.

At some time in pre-recorded history, we decided to move out of our caves and merge with other people into ever larger units. We figured out how to make tools that could manipulate and shape nature how we wanted it to be (this was crucial for the later invention of rounder balls, harder clubs, and smoother playing fields). We created towns and villages. The first societies were born.

Accompanying those developments was the development of two critical characteristics of settled life: (1) material prosperity, which allows us to have leisure time, and (2) physical security, which gives us the confidence to plan for the future—we could now imagine a future—and work on projects that might take some time to complete. After all, it would be fruitless to build a golf course if it could be destroyed at any moment by a neighboring tribe.

Eventually, we created enough of the luxuries of life and had established a sufficient sense of security and confidence in the reality of a future that we could turn our amazing imagination to the finer things in life. And so, organized sport was born.

At the same time that we had the leisure to play organized games, we had the time to reflect on the world we had created. Since we had the time to teach our children to play games, we also had the time to educate them, to teach them about reading and writing, the difference between right and wrong, as well as the history and traditions of our society. In other words, philosophy and sport developed simultaneously, when we had the leisure time and sense of security to do both.

Now that we understand the long link between sports and philosophy, let us return to the most cerebral and contemplative of sports: the game of golf.

We can only play golf because we can think. Indeed, golf would be impossible to play without highly developed brains. In order to play, we must understand mathematics in order to keep score and calculate distances; we must understand physics in order to select clubs, determine trajectories and evaluate the slopes of greens; we must understand the natural world in order to assess how the angle of the sun and the growth rate of grass might affect our putts; we must calculate risks and rewards in order to decide what shot to attempt; we must reflect on our own physical capabilities in order to make the right shot-making decisions; we must be psychologically astute in order to ensure that our emotions help and do not harm our performance; we must be able to comprehend the value of abstract ideas such as rules, etiquette, and fairness in order to play without being assessed penalties.

Furthermore, as anyone who has analyzed a terrible round knows, we think because we play golf. Golf is perhaps the only sport that provides such an endless source of self-analysis. Every shot in a round can be replayed in our minds over and over. Different decisions could have been made, different shots played, different clubs chosen, different strategies employed—oh, how we could have improved our score if only we had made another decision!

Since golf is the most cerebral of games, it is only natural and right to compare it to the most cerebral of intellectual pursuits: philosophy. As we embark on a history of Western philosophy, don't forget that reading about the greatest thoughts of the greatest thinkers in human history will inevitably improve your performance on the course.

Introduction to Golf Instruction

Bruce Loome

HAVING been a devoted teacher of this wonderful game for twenty years, I am writing in order to provide golf instruction, which will stand alongside Dr. Sola's philosophical history and will create a direct relationship between philosophy and modern golf instruction.

All of the chapters will be accompanied by a section labeled *Golf Tip*. The tips will help you to implement on the golf course some key concepts drawn from the philosophy sections. As they often focus on the mental game, these tips will help you manage your own thoughts and feelings on the course.

Just as philosophy is built upon core principles about knowledge, truth and reality, golf is built upon fundamentals:

grip, stance, posture, alignment, and aiming. In Chapter 3, "The Platonic Golfer," you will see these concepts in sections titled *Golf Fundamentals*. Looking back over the fundamentals during your reading will help you not only learn, but also understand the key elements of a sound golf swing.

Lastly, the lessons throughout this book will sometimes be accompanied by anecdotes and true stories from the world of golf, titled *Golf History*. I have been very fortunate over the last twelve years to work for Tiger Woods and, more recently, Darren Clarke at the British Open. I have been able to observe closely some of the best players to ever have played the game manage the ups-and-downs of high pressure rounds on some of the most difficult courses in England and Scotland. These stories will help you understand how to make key decisions in difficult moments in your rounds.

All of these helpful hints together will give you a better understanding of the swing, a clearer connection between better practice and better play, a stronger control over your own thoughts, and a fuller conception of the virtues of great golfers. At the end of this book, you will play better golf and enjoy this fantastic game even more.

1 THE PRE-SOCRATIC GOLFER

GOLF began in Scotland, and philosophy began in ancient Greece.

These claims ring true to the Western ear, but they merit closer scrutiny. Just as the Dutch might object to golf's Scottish origin, both Indian and Chinese people might object to ancient Greece's distinction as the originator of human thought. After all, both Lao Tzu and Confucius in China as well as the Buddha in India were producing philosophy in the 5th century BC. At roughly the same time, early Greek thinkers such as Heraclitus and Parmenides were laying the foundations for Western thought.

Golf might have originated from the Dutch sport of *kolf*, which was played with sticks and a ball on frozen canals. From the Netherlands, the sport was transferred by Dutch merchants and sailors to Scotland, some seven or eight hundred years ago. The Scots then adapted *kolf* to the land-based game that we know today.

References to "the golfe" began to appear in the fifteenth century with King James II banning the game in 1457 for it being one of the "unprofitable sportes" along with football or soccer. The first historical reference to the links at St. Andrews appeared in 1552. One Archbishop Hamilton decreed that the land should be filled with rabbits and also be spared from development so golfers could play their matches. Still, the game of golf was not strictly regulated. Only in 1744 were the first 13 rules of golf established, and only in 1764 did the Old Course at St. Andrews adopt the now standard 18-hole format. In short, this magnificent ball-and-stick sport evolved slowly over time from its mysterious origins to what we now know as the modern game of golf.

The origins of philosophy are just as complex, obscure and mysterious. The isolated cultures of Ancient Greece, China and India were all developing philosophy simultaneously, so it is difficult to determine specifically where philosophy originated. However, most scholars agree that what we now know as philosophy in the Western tradition began in ancient Greece.

Socrates is often considered to be the father of Western philosophy, although he was not the first. Most students of philosophy regard Thales of Miletus (c. 7th-6th century BC) to be the very first philosopher, and he lived about two hundred years before Socrates. Thales and the other thinkers who came before Socrates are collectively known as the pre-Socratics.

The pre-Socratics were the first natural philosophers; they

devoted their energy to discovering *physis* (from which we get the word physics) or the fundamental nature of the universe. As these early philosophers in ancient Greece observed the world, they noticed natural phenomena changing in many ways. For example, water becomes steam and then seemingly disappears. Fire breaks out spontaneously and consumes what it touches, leaving different matter (ashes) behind. Plants, animals, and human beings grow, and sometimes they shrink, decompose and disappear. How does all of this happen? How does stuff become other stuff? How can it change, grow, shrink, burn, or disappear? How do balls fly through the air? Is the air a void? Or is it just a fluid we cannot see? Does it change when something passes through it?

Trying to figure out the answers to these questions was the first goal of these early thinkers, who, since they were studying nature, are also called natural philosophers.

The first thinkers came up with some odd theories about the nature of the universe. However, we can forgive them for their strange beliefs because there were no experienced professionals to guide them. Thales, for example, asserted that the fundamental substance of the universe was water. The other pre-Socratic thinkers who came after him, including Pythagoras and Empedocles, proposed other ideas to explain the fundamental nature of the universe. For example, Pythagoras, the great mathematician, insisted that all things in the world are actually numbers. Empedocles believed that the universe was made of four substances: earth, air, fire and water.

Two more early philosophers, Leucippus of Miletus and Democritus of Abdera, actually formulated a very modern version of our understanding of the universe. They proposed the existence of atoms, indivisible particles that permanently exist and that can be combined in various ways to make the world we live in.

All of the pre-Socratics provide much food for thought; in this chapter, however, we will look at only two of the most important pre-Socratic thinkers: Heraclitus and Parmenides.

Heraclitus of Ionia

"Everything flows; nothing remains."

The goal of the early pre-Socratics was to explain the fundamental nature of the universe given their observations about the natural world. Specifically, however, they wanted to determine if the change we see is real or if it's an illusion. Let's see why this question matters, and where you stand on this issue by asking a straight-forward question about golf: Have you ever played the same golf course twice?

You might think this a silly question. Of course, we play the same golf courses, some over and over again. Many of us have played our club course or local public course dozens if not hundreds of times.

Alas, Heraclitus (c. 5th century BC) would think you are misguided. He would say that we never play the same course twice, and he has a point. If what we mean by "the same course" is exactly the same course, then we never do. After all, even if we play the same course twice in the same day, it is not the same. From hour to hour, the grass is growing ever so slightly; the wind is blowing in imperceptibly different strengths and directions; the grains of sand in the bunker, even when perfectly raked, will never be exactly where they were before; the divots in the fairway will be filled, but the resulting turf is not exactly the same as it was before. More obviously, the pin positions change as do the tee boxes, so even if we play the same course in a certain general sense, it is never really the same. From this reasoning, Heraclitus drew the conclusion that only change is real. As he said, "You can never put your foot in the same river twice."

Of course, understanding that the same course is never really the same is critical for golfers who want to lower their scores.

Golf Tip: The Heraclitean Golfer

Let us now apply Heraclitus' important concept—that nothing ever is the same—to your golf game, specifically how changing course conditions change the game. A good understanding of how course conditions affect how the ball flies is vital both during a round and between rounds.

This will enable you to continue that good score and not let the change in conditions ruin your score and weaken your concentration. There are very obvious changes during and between rounds—changes in wind, temperature and rain—and dealing with these factors is essential. All of these elements can make the ball travel more or less distance both in the air and on the roll. Being aware of these elements allows the player to make clubbing decisions or even swing adjustments to combat some or all of these possible changes.

Common mistakes that amateurs make with regards to changing conditions are sometimes due to complacency and over-familiarity with their local course. If a player hits a 7 iron into a par 3 on the local course on a weekly basis, he or she will tend to pull the 7 from the bag without really taking into consideration the change in conditions, i.e. wind strength, temperature, and dampness. These elements can have a severe effect on ball flight and trajectory, hence giving the ball a different optimum distance of travel.

Wind: Wind can affect the ball flight immensely no matter what direction it is coming from. Playing down wind the ball can be "knocked down," which means that it will not reach its true height or trajectory. In this case, the wind influences not only the distance the ball travels but also the angle at which the ball is approaching the green or target. A lower ball flight onto the green will mean that the ball will have less back spin and will need longer to stop. A good example of when this is important is if the flag is towards the back of the green and *the wind is behind. You can afford to land the ball shorter than the flag's position, allowing for the extra roll that the lower trajectory will produce. If the ball was hit more pin-high, then the chances of holding the green and not going over the back, leaving a difficult chip, are remote at best.*

If you are playing into the wind, then there is a much better prospect for getting the ball close to the pin. Remember, we may have to hit one or even two clubs more to allow for the distance taken off by the wind, but this direction of the wind can afford us the luxury of being positive and somewhat aggressive with our shot getting the ball to land beyond the pin, knowing there is a very good possibility of the ball spinning back towards the hole.

Cross winds are probably the hardest of the wind shots to deal with. Judging the amount to allow either left or right takes a great deal of skill, practice and commitment. However, the main factor to consider is commitment! Once you have allowed for the wind and selected your new target, you must commit to the new target. It is all too common for amateurs to aim at the new target and yet not commit 100 percent to that target. They then try to "help" the ball back on line! The result is never good.

Temperature: *Temperature can also have a direct effect on the distance the ball travels. During the summer months and especially in hot climates, the ball will travel some 10 percent farther due to the increase in air temperature and the decrease in air density as the ball* gains height. This can have dramatic consequences when hitting approach shots into the green if the allowance of the extra travel has not been figured into the shot. Also the warmer days produce firmer, faster running fairways resulting in more roll—something to consider when ensuring you avoid the fairway bunkers.

Professional golfers (or their caddies) often carry another ball—same make, compression and marking—in their pocket during a round in colder climates to ensure that they can alternate the ball for each hole. The ball not in use can be warmed up ready for the subsequent hole. Doing the same will help you feel comfortable in colder weather.

Rain: Rain will have an effect on ball flight, but not that much, unless rain is combined with wind. Allowances have to be made more for the greens on rainy days. The best players and those playing on the world stage will welcome the rain as it will soften the greens and allow the players to take dead aim at the flags knowing that the amount of spin will be reduced greatly.

However, for those club golfers playing in the monthly medal, remember that the rain can have an effect on the putting surfaces, making them aquaplane initially and then pull up short due to the drag from the surface water. During the day the greens may begin to dry out and start to speed up again—something to be mindful of during your round.

During the 2011 Open Championship I was very fortunate to accompany Darren Clarke during his victorious final round at St

George's in Kent. Bad weather plagued the tournament, and it was no coincidence that the players who accepted the weather and decided to treat it as yet another challenge, in addition to the course and the competition, faired the best. Darren played the final round in much the same way as the previous three, with a smile and a fantastic attitude. Some of the other world class players did complain and curse the weather conditions, but there really is not a great deal anyone can do about the weather.

In order to ensure you play your best in adverse conditions, dress appropriately, have enough dry gloves and towels with you and go and do battle, but this time not just with yourself and the course, but also the ever-changing course conditions and elements.

Parmenides of Elea

"It is necessary to say and think that being is; for to be is possible, and nothingness is not possible."

Heraclitus insisted that change alone was the only truth. What we think is the same golf course is really always different. Our experience of changing course conditions shows us the truth of his belief.

However, Parmenides (c. 5th century BC) disagreed with Heraclitus. Parmenides believed that all change is an illusion—

nothing changes. We only think things change because our senses seem to tell us so, but our senses deceive us. In other words, our local golf course is always the same course, despite what appear to be changing course conditions or different pin placements.

Parmenides' argument stems from the approach that all things must exist because nothingness cannot exist. We cannot say that nothing becomes something or that something becomes nothing. The conclusion is that no change can happen. All somethings are always what they are, because they cannot become what they are not.

The important point here is that Parmenides was the first to tell people that what seems to be the truth is not necessarily true. And this might be one truth of all philosophers—they are the only people who insist that our common sense and most entrenched ideas about the world might just be false. Philosophers are often unpopular for just this reason.

So, a golf course cannot become what it is not. If the golf course can become something else, then it was never a golf course to begin with because change implies turning "something that is" into "something that is not." Things that don't exist cannot exist; something cannot come from nothing, nor can nothing come from something. Parmenides insisted, "If something comes into being, it is not; nor is it if it is going to be in the future."

In short, strict Parmenidean logic tells us that the golf course was always a golf course and will always be one, and that we play the same one over and over again. In fact, Parmenides would insist that all golf courses are actually the same course! Our senses might tell us differently, but those senses are wrong.

What insight about golf can we draw from the idea that all courses might actually be the same or, at the very least, approached in the same way?

Golf Tip: The Parmenidean Golfer

In theory, treating every course as the same course could help tremendously with your mental frailties during local tournaments or matches at other courses. Each game is just another game of golf, right? It is the same game you play each week on your own course. The rules are the same, the clubs are the same, and the shots need to be executed in the same way. In this sense, each course is the same.

Playing the "same" course in your head will help to alleviate some of the new pressures that manifest themselves on pastures new, but this is extremely difficult to do for 18 holes. Sooner or later you will let your guard down and then the pressures and anxieties of playing a new course, with many new hazards, may in fact seem greater than they would have originally.

When preparing to play a new course or, in fact, a round on your own course, try to analyze which holes you have a realistic chance to par or birdie and which holes you probably will only bogey. Remember that unless your handicap is 0 or below, there are holes out there where a bogey is more than acceptable. Too many handicapped players are trying to play this game as a tour star. This can be terribly frustrating and can lead from one bad hole to another—and another. Get used to playing within yourself and to your handicap. If you are given a stroke on the hole, use it! Play conservatively instead of using your extra stroke to chip out of the woods.

Very few, if any, tour pros approach any course in the same way. Depending on conditions, they are able to execute the shot in a multitude of different ways to get the best result. However, they do try to play each shot the same way. All the best golfers in the world have a pre-shot routine. This can comprise of standing back and analyzing the shot required, stepping forward into the hitting area, addressing the ball and finally making the shot.

Having a pre-shot routine not only reduces anxiety but can also give you the feeling that you are doing the same thing over and over again. By having the same routine for every shot, we can trick our minds into thinking that we are playing the same shot or course over and over again. Try getting your own pre-shot routine and ensure that you use this each and every time you play a shot on any and every course. After a short time, the routine will feel very natural and will allow your mind and body to settle into the routine prior to each shot, reducing anxiety and stress, freeing up your swing, and producing much *more consistent ball-striking.*

Conclusion

Just like the first kolfers and the first golfers, the pre-Socratics are important because they were the first to experiment with something new. The first golfers were creating the foundation for the modern game of golf, and the first philosophers were beginning to establish our modern, scientific understanding of the world.

Of course, both the early golfers and the early philosophers made some wrong turns. For example, the Old Course at St. Andrews was originally a 22-hole loop of twelve total holes, ten of which were played twice. The round was divided into an outward and inward eleven. Of course, golfers going on the outward eleven would necessarily meet groups coming in, which led to some problems with ball identification and playing rights. These problems were eventually solved with the creation of double greens with different pins, so groups would not clash. Four holes were combined into two, making a total of ten holes, eight being played twice—the origin of the 18-hole course.

Just as the modern 18-hole course was developed through trial and error, so the early philosophers made mistakes in their theories about the nature of the universe. However, they were important because they were the first to ask questions about the nature of reality. Heraclitus insisted that change alone was real, and Parmenides insisted that nothing ever changed.

Neither of these positions is necessarily true, but they do help us understand two key points about golf. First, there are benefits to being a Heraclitean golfer. We ought to remember that even our local course is never really the same course. Innumerable factors weigh on our shot-making decisions. Course conditions should always influence our approach to every shot. At the same time, there are benefits to being a Paremenidian golfer. We ought to develop a pre-shot routine, a way to approach every shot the same way, regardless of the course, hole, conditions or competitive circumstances. When we approach every shot with the same routine, we develop a sense of comfort that helps us maintain our confidence in ourselves and our mastery over our swing.

.

2 THE SOCRATIC GOLFER

"Know thyself!"

—The Oracle at Delphi

SOCRATES said that we call a man a carpenter if he has learned the art of carpentry, a musician if he has learned the art of music, and a doctor if he has learned the art of medicine. However, we would not call a carpenter good if his furniture breaks, a musician good if he can't carry a tune, or a doctor good if he kills his patients. So, too, we will call a golfer one who has learned the art of golf, but we will not call him good if he scores in the 120s. He is a hacker, not a golfer.

However, the hacker might still insist he is a golfer, despite sound and rational objections to the contrary. How did this happen? How can the hacker insist he is a golfer, despite the fact that he is really bad at golf?

We can blame the Sophists for his stubbornness.

From the Pre-Socratics to the Sophists

We remember from the last chapter that Heraclitus believed in change and Parmenides did not, and we might be frustrated by their dispute. Why does it matter if we can prove that change does or does not exist? Well, many ancient Greeks felt the same way about these disputes about the nature of the universe. The cynical philosopher Diogenes, after patiently listening to the argument that change does not exist, simply got up and walked away—proving his point rather well.

You also might be thinking that these pre-Socratic philosophers are out of touch with the problems that affect real people living real lives. Indeed, philosophy is often irritating, difficult and frustrating because it deals with problems that aren't problems at all. Intellectual disputes about "the nature of reality" are not practical. They do not help us live in this world.

Similar theoretical debates plague the world of golf. If you spend a lot of time reading golf magazines and watching golf on TV, you are bound to hear many different opinions about golf technique. One pro tells you to do one thing to improve your chipping, and another tells you to do the opposite. One pro says focus on your takeaway, and the other says focus on your swing plane. As a result of so much conflicting information, you might be inclined to ignore all of the contradictory professional advice and stick with whatever works for you.

As a result of too much abstract, impractical and contradictory philosophy, a new school of philosophers arose in Greece in the 5th century BC to meet the need for a philosophy that was useful for normal people living normal lives: these thinkers were the Sophists, whose name derives from the Greek word *sophos* (wise), from which we also derive the word *philosophy* (the love of wisdom).

The Sophists were roving thinkers who travelled around ancient Greece from city to city, educating people for a price. They were the first professional educators in the Western world. They made education very much what it is today: an institution that teaches people how to succeed in the world. They taught the skills that any Greek needed to become wealthy, powerful and influential, skills such as rhetoric, the art of persuasive public speaking.

The pre-Socratics developed one of the great themes of philosophy—*physis*, or the study of the universe. The Sophists, in reaction, developed a second central theme in philosophy—the study of the human condition.

What might strike us as strange about the Sophists is how they framed their goals. For example, the goal of rhetoric was not to find the truth. The truth did not matter to them. In any argument, all that matters is winning, even if the winning position is actually false. A successful public speaker is one who convinces his audience that his position is right, even if in truth his position is wrong. This is a startling new development in thought. Instead of focusing on the discovery of truth, as the pre-Socratics wished to do about the natural world, the Sophists insisted that we should only focus on successful outcomes. This attitude to success—defined as getting your way or convincing other people you are right, regardless of the truth—was one of the prime values of the Sophists, a value that they thought would lead to a happy and rewarding life. This turning away from truth, in favor of winning, was a remarkable development in Western thought.

Protagoras and Relativism

"Of all things the measure is man…No one thinks falsely, and you, whether you will or not, must be a measure."

Like many Sophists, Protagoras (481-411 BC) approached knowledge by making the simple observation that different people and different societies have different, often contradictory beliefs. For example, Parmenides didn't believe in change, but Heraclitus did. Some barbarian tribes like the Callatians ate their dead, but the Greeks burned theirs. A person with stomach flu thinks a filet mignon is disgusting, but a healthy person thinks it is delicious. You might believe that swinging as hard as you can will increase your distance, but your friend tells you that you should probably just relax. You might also believe that gripping the putter tighter will increase your accuracy, but a pro on TV tells you this is wrong.

Who is right on these matters? Well, Protagoras made the observation that no one is ever right or wrong about anything. The truth is what we make of it. If we convince other people that our own personal truth is the Truth, then we win.

Indeed, Protagoras was one of the very first philosophers who insisted that no one is necessarily right or wrong about anything that they truly believe. What matters is what appears to be true for each of us. When he said that "man is the measure of all things," he meant that each of us as individuals decides what is true and what is false. There is no independent, objective standard of truth. The Callatians aren't wrong for eating their dead. They think it is right; therefore, it is. You aren't wrong for swinging your driver like a battle axe. You think it is right; therefore, it is.

This idea about right and wrong, truth and falsehood, being decided by individuals is called relativism, and it is one of the most influential ideas in the history of Western philosophy.

This way of approaching the truth or lack of truth in the real world is similar to how many people approach the truth or lack of truth in the world of golf. Many golfers believe in playing the game their own way, with no help from anyone. After all, whatever works, they truly believe, has to work for them.

A professional golf instructor, of course, would have some serious objections to this approach.

Golf Tip: The Sophist Golfer

Many weekend golfers I see on the course are Sophists. They insist that there is no truth. They grip the club in their own way, swing wildly according to their own style, and break every rule of golf imaginable. They refuse to take lessons because they refuse to believe that there is a truth to the matter.

When advised to take lessons in order to learn the fundamentals, they rightly point out that Tour players do things their own way—the pros are Sophists too! For example, Jim Furyk does seem to have a very individual swing; however, the truth is that during impact he is technically and fundamentally sound.

Golf instruction can really be terribly confusing if we listen to many different pros, read lots of different articles, or watch more than our fair share of instruction videos. This confusion can be better understood if we remember what the Sophists would say: "We all have our own truth."

The Sophists' attitude—that what must work, must work for you—is often accurate. However, some principles still have to work for everyone. Being more relaxed during the swing, keeping your eye on the ball longer, and having a balanced and full follow-through must work for everyone. It is true that some of the best players in the world look as though their swings differ, and of course they do. However, throughout the PGA and European Tours, you would be hard pressed to find a touring professional who does not possess mastery of the five fundamentals: 1. Grip 2. Stance 3. Posture 4. Alignment 5. Aiming.

Even the best pros focus on these concepts day-in and day-out. I have spent countless hours on the practice ground at the British Open watching the best hundred professionals in the world hitting ball after ball down the range, and whenever one of them seems to be having a little difficulty, the pro always goes to his coach! They will then review the fundamentals together. Throughout my time to date working for Tiger, he has had only a few coaches—Butch Harman, Hank Haney, and now Sean Foley—but no matter who seems to be the man of the moment they all concentrate on ensuring the fundamentals are in place.

Another terrific example of a golfer who devotes himself to the fundamentals is Viijay Singh, who is also an avid and organized practicer. He goes through the fundamentals and swing path in detail constantly. He grooves these important parts of the swing so that under pressure the swing mechanics hold up and he can perform well when it matters most—when he's in a position to win tournaments.

*

The Sophists' contribution to philosophy was to remind us that often there is no such thing as right and wrong, truth and falsehood. All that manners is being successful, winning. The relativist golfer insists there is no necessary truth that would lead to a better swing or a longer drive even though the professional instructor insists that there are some fundamentals which really are true. If sloppy technique helps us win golf matches, who is anyone to judge our style?

Of course, it is no use to argue with the relativist golfer. He would just remind us that whatever he does works for him, and that's all there is to it.

Even though the Sophists insisted that a relativist approach was the correct way to deal with disputes about both right and wrong as well as truth and falsehood and even though they insisted that all that matters is winning, this approach might not actually lead to success, either in life or on the course. Believing that the murder is right or that the earth is flat might not actually lead to a happy life. Similarly, believing that we can ignore the fundamentals might not actually lower our golf scores.

Perhaps there are truths in this world, truths that make us both happy in our private lives and successful on the links. We just need a great mind to show us what we need to do in order to discover them.

Old Tom and Socrates

When we think of greatness in any human endeavor, there are those who are commonly regarded as being truly great. One early golfer and one early philosopher embody all that is truly great and good about both their professions and also human beings in general. One is Old Tom Morris and the other is Socrates.

The Scotsman Old Tom (1820-1908) is often considered to be the father of golf. How to begin with his achievements? He was a great organizer, a tremendous player, an astute technological innovator, a revolutionary course architect, and a good man. He helped to found the Open Championship in 1860, and he won it himself four times. He was the head greenskeeper at both Prestwick and St. Andrews, where he pioneered the use of the lawnmower as well as metal cups for pins. He designed a number of courses himself and introduced new concepts in course design, such as the creation of hazards to force players to make strategic shot-making decisions. This innovation, of course, turned golf into the game of strategy that we play today.

Without Old Tom's dedication to the game, golf would not be the intellectual challenge that it is. He did not accept the "truths" of golf that were handed down to him. Because he was open-minded, he was able to discover new truths of golf that have shaped our understanding of the modern game.

Socrates (c. 470 BC—399 BC) is no less important to

philosophy than Old Tom is to golf. The great Athenian is widely considered to be the father of Western philosophy. Just as Old Tom shaped our understanding of golf, so Socrates has shaped our understanding of what is good and true in human life. Indeed, when we think of philosophy, the first name that comes to mind is Socrates.

We know a great deal about Socrates and his ideas, but not through his own writings. Socrates wrote very little, so our only knowledge of him comes by way of his student Plato. What we do know from Plato is that he was quite ugly, but also that he commanded the respect of all of his friends and fellow citizens because of his courage, moderation, wit and wisdom.

Regarding his courage, no one disputed that he was one of the bravest soldiers in the Athenian army. His confidence and fearlessness made most enemy soldiers steer clear of him. In one battle, he was the only soldier willing to put himself in great danger to rescue a wounded comrade. Then, when offered a medal for valor, he insisted that it be given to the wounded man he rescued.

Regarding his moderation, he advocated living a life of frugality, paying more attention to one's own virtue than to money, power or status. He insisted that the virtuous man would be the happiest in the long run. He avoided most common pleasures, and abstained from sex and excessive food and drink.

His wit often appeared in jokes about his own lack of good looks, although he could also use it to attack and undermine the philosophical pretensions of his opponents.

For his wisdom, however, is he most worthy of our praise.

The Wisdom of Socrates

"The unexamined life is not worth living."

Socrates could be considered a Sophist philosopher himself, because he was a professional educator living in the era of the Sophists. However, unlike the Sophists, he refused to charge a fee for his instruction. After all, Socrates insisted that he wanted to teach people how to become virtuous and excellent. It was enough reward for Socrates to make life-long friends who became good people as a result of his instruction.

Socrates was also different from the Sophists because he rejected the idea of relativism. Justice, wisdom and excellence were not just what any individual believed they might be. Indeed, since a doctor could not consider himself to be excellent if he kills all of his patients, we cannot consider ourselves to be just or wise if we are mean and stupid. Socrates insisted that we could establish things to be the truth, given the proper philosophical approach: (1) we have to recognize what we do not know and (2) we have to be open to changing our minds.

Socrates' special contribution to philosophy was precisely a unique way of seeking the truth called the Socratic method. This method involves the teacher asking questions and forcing the student to answer them. As the student answers more and more questions, he finds out the truth for himself. This was important for Socrates, who believed that the educator should be a "midwife" to the truth. In other words, a good teacher should help people discover the truth themselves, without doing it for them, in the same way that a midwife helps a mother give birth, without giving birth herself.

Similarly, Socrates was humble about his own wisdom. Rather than insisting he knew a lot, he insisted the opposite; this alone made him wise. As he said of one of his philosophical opponents in the *Apology*:

> ...he thinks he knows something when he does not, whereas when I do not know, neither do I think I know; so I am likely to be wiser than he to this small extent, that I do not think I know what I do not know.

For Socrates, accepting the limits of our knowledge is the first step to being wise.

The second step requires having the right attitude towards self-improvement. Not everyone is necessarily a good student, especially if they are interested in the Sophist value of winning at all costs—at the expense of the truth. Socrates insisted that the correct approach to knowledge is to focus exclusively on discovering the truth. This means that a good student must be open to criticism and open to changing his mind.

Indeed, in order to be excellent at any endeavor, we must

believe that it is possible to become better and to learn more. Compare this attitude to the Sophist's insistence that there is no such thing as better or worse, truth or falsehood. Socrates would argue that this Sophistical attitude towards knowledge will lead us to become worse not better people.

When Socrates insists that the unexamined life is not worth living, he is saying that we need to have the right attitude towards our lives. We need to want to know who we are, our strengths and weaknesses. In order to do so, we need to be willing learners and willing questioners.

So, too, if we want to be better golfers, we need to be willing to examine our game and have the right attitude towards changing it. This attitude is critical when deciding to become a better golfer. Just as the youth of Athens sought out Socrates in order to become better people, so we too should seek out a pro in order to become better golfers. Crucially, we need to have the right attitude when we seek out the truth of golf.

Golf Tip: The Socratic Golfer

Many casual golfers never look at the fundamentals or take lessons. However, if casual golfers do decide to take lessons, they are inevitably frustrated when the lesson makes them feel uncomfortable with their normal swing. Often, they will even play worse for some time. Their temporary lack of success reinforces their Sophistical belief that there is no truth to golf. As Socrates would say, this is the wrong attitude to have about your quest to become a better golfer.

It is crucial to have the right attitude when embarking on a series of lessons. Learning a new technique is difficult. I spend a great deal of time telling my clients that it is not that difficult, but of course we all know it is—a little positive psychology never hurt anyone!

There is a very good possibility that during the lessons the golfer may feel as though he or she is taking one step forward and two back; this is a normal feeling and one that the pro should prepare the golfer to expect. However, it is not really happening this way; the new feelings are normally quite different from the ones they already have, and therefore it takes some time to settle in and start to feel the new mechanics.

What then tends to happen is that during the lesson, whilst having continual instruction and support, the lesson takes effect and the ball flight improves and the golfer is happy. However, after leaving the lesson bay, if not enough time is allowed to engrain the new feelings, then the golfer will attempt to take this lesson onto the course. The new techniques will work for a short time, but without the hours spent practicing, they will naturally begin to falter and then the golfer will tend to revert back to what felt comfortable. This is the worst of places to be in. Some of the new swing and a lot of the old. A combination of the two is not conducive to good golf, and the golfer will feel that the lesson has not worked. This, of course, is not strictly true. Any lesson will take a lot of practice and commitment to engrain into your muscles and replace some of the other, incorrect actions that have been part of the swing for some time before. The easy option would be to go back to the Sophist's idea of "what works for you." I would implore you not to do this. If you have taken the time and parted with the money to seek professional help, then give the lessons some time to take effect. Work together with your pro and practice as hard as you can. I promise you that with the right instruction and the right amount of time and effort, the lessons will help your game and improve your scores.

The Death of Socrates

Like Old Tom Morris, Socrates lived to a ripe old age, but unlike Old Tom, he did not die of natural causes. Accused of corrupting the youth of Athens by not respecting the old gods, Socrates was given the death sentence, which he carried out himself by drinking hemlock.

Even though the charges against Socrates were false, he had annoyed too many Athenians in his life to have a sympathetic jury. Indeed, in his defense, Socrates reminded the jury that he spent much of his life telling them, his fellow citizens, that they were not as wise as they thought they were, and that their wealth and status did not mean they were good people:

> What do I deserve to suffer or to pay because I have deliberately not led a quiet life but have neglected what occupies most people: wealth, household affairs, the position of general or public orator or the other offices, the political clubs and factions that exist in the city? I thought myself too honest to survive if I occupied myself with those things....
> [Instead] I went to each of you privately and conferred upon you what I say is the greatest benefit, by trying to persuade you not to care for any of his belongings before caring that you yourself should be as good and as wise as possible.

Instead of apologizing, which might have led to his acquittal, he persisted in pointing out their hypocrisy and wickedness, no matter what the consequences—including death:

> I will not yield to any man contrary to what is right, for fear of death, even if I should die at once for not yielding.... As long as I draw breath and am able, I shall not cease to practice philosophy.

So the jury did sentence Socrates to death; it was a death he chose freely, a death he accepted without complaint.

Nearly everyone who came in contact with him learned to respect him. Even the prison officer who guarded him during his imprisonment told Socrates, with tears in his eyes, on the final day of his life, "During the time you have been here [in prison], I have come to know you as the noblest, gentlest, and the best man who has ever come here." This sentiment was echoed by Plato, who wrote that Socrates "was of all those we have known, the best, and also the wisest and the most upright."

Conclusion

Humans tend to be inflexible in many ways. We refuse to change our minds about our beliefs. We hold to our political views no matter what. We stick to our moral beliefs no matter what. We refuse to change. We are not necessarily wrong by being so inflexible. After all, there are so many voices telling us so many different things that it is easiest to settle into our own beliefs and reject anyone who criticizes us. The Sophists insisted that it was good to be inflexible about our beliefs—to deny that there is truth. Whatever we believe to be the case is the case. Man is, as Protagoras insisted, the measure of all things.

The Sophist golfer is no different. He insists that his swing is the right swing. It works for him, and he refuses to accept any advice that contradicts his beliefs. He insists he is a golfer even though he is a hacker.

And this is why Socrates is important: he was the first to challenge the Sophist's attitude to knowledge and self-improvement. If we want to be good people, we must be willing to accept our lack of knowledge and we must be ready to change our minds. Furthermore, we must have the right attitude. We must want to find the truth, even if it contradicts all of our beliefs.

The good student of golf, the Socratic golfer, must have the right attitude to the game. He must be willing to assess his strengths and weaknesses, be open to new ideas, and listen to the advice of good golfers, who are proven to be good by their mastery of the game. If he does this, his scores will improve. As his scores improve and as he continues to learn the art of golf, he will cease being a hacker. He will become a true golfer.

3 THE PLATONIC GOLFER

*"The true lover of knowledge naturally strives for truth,
and is not content with common opinion,
but soars with undimmed and unwearied passion
until he grasps the essential nature of things."*

—Plato, *The Republic* (c. 375 BC)

SWING. The perfect swing. If there is one thing for which all avid golfers strive, it is the perfect swing. The concept of the perfect swing is a strange idea, because some golfers seem to play pretty well without anything approaching a good swing, let alone a perfect one. Even excellent golfers with fundamentally sound swings have quirks that prevent them from having perfect swings. So, does the perfect swing really exist? Can we actually discover what it is? And, by doing so, can we actually improve our game?

Before looking at the idea of the perfect swing in a

philosophical fashion, let's recap the previous chapters in which we learned about the pre-Socratics the Sophists.

Heraclitus insisted that the world is constantly changing and that nothing ever stays the same. He would argue that we can never play the same golf course twice, because every time we play what we think is the same course, it has changed in subtle ways (the wind has changed direction, the grass has grown, etc.).

Parmenides, however, insisted that nothing ever changes, even though our senses suggest they do. Although our senses constantly deceive us, reason, logic, and mathematics never do. These things never change.

Enter the Sophists who said that disputes about the nature of reality are merely a waste of time.

Sophists like Protagoras proposed the doctrine of relativism: truth is subjective, which is to say it is determined by the individual. Heraclitus can believe what he wants, Parmenides can believe what he wants, and you can believe what you want. All beliefs are equal. As the great Sophist Protagoras reminds us, *no one thinks falsely*.

Returning to golf, if I am happy with my ugly swing, if it works for me, I don't need some instructor telling me that it is ugly and ineffective and that I should change it. These instructors are like Heraclitus, Parmenides and Zeno. They are dogmatic. They think there is really a right way and a wrong way to swing. The experienced Sophist reminds us, however, that what is right one day is wrong the next—what is right for Tiger is wrong for Phil.

It is now time for Plato (c. 427-348 BC)—the rich, powerful and brilliant son of a distinguished Athenian family—to enter the debate. Plato lived during a time of great turmoil in Athens and lived under many different forms of government. He was disgusted by *all* of them. He bemoaned the fact that it seemed that those best suited to rule never actually ruled. It seemed, to the contrary, that the most persuasive or most popular or most affluent people led, but never the best. In an effort to change this, he began to write and teach in the hopes that he could conclusively determine what the best society would be like. This project culminated in *The Republic*, which is as important to philosophers as Ben Hogan's *Modern Fundamentals* is to golfers. Indeed, Plato will prove conclusively that you should listen to your pro and change your ugly swing.

Plato's Argument

In order to create the best republic, Plato had to destroy the Sophists' idea that truth is relative. After all, their idea leads inevitably to the conclusion that there can be no such thing as a "better" or "worse" government. A tyranny would be "good" for the tyrant and his cronies, but "bad" for his victims. A monarchy would be "good" for the monarch and his family, but "bad" for everyone else. If relativism is correct, no such thing as a "just" and "wise" government could ever exist.

Remember, the Sophists believe that no one thinks falsely. Following this idea, if the truth is relative, there can be no such thing as a "good" or "bad" golf swing. If the truth is relative, then all you need to do is truly believe that your bad swing is perfect and—*voila!*—you've attained the perfect swing.

Other people might believe your swing is a bad swing, of course, but it's no use arguing with them.

Sophists acknowledge that people disagree, but there really is no truth to the matter. The problem Plato faced about creating a good government is the same problem that golfers face. If truth is relative, then we might as well abandon all of our efforts to improve our swings.

So how did Plato restore our faith in objective truth, and by extension prove that there can be both a better government and a better golf swing?

Well, a person with stomach flu thinks steaks are disgusting, but a healthy person thinks they are tasty. Therefore, the Sophists claim there is no truth in the matter. It would be silly to call a sick person ignorant for not knowing the truth about steaks.

Plato would respond as follows: Steaks being tasty is a matter of opinion, *but not all questions are matters of opinion.* For example, you might think the Earth is flat, and I might think it is round, but from this we do not draw the conclusion that there is no truth about the shape of the Earth. Indeed, the roundness of the Earth is not a matter of opinion like steaks being tasty. We can establish its roundness with reason and empirical observation.

The Four Types of Truth

Plato concludes that there are different types of truths: the truths of subjective opinion (relative truths) and the truths of demonstrable fact (objective truths). These truths combine in four distinct ways.

Let's say you are travelling and want to reach your destination.

(1) You can be a blind man on the wrong road. This is no good. You believe you are on the right road, but you're on the wrong road, and you're blind so you can't even discover that you are on the wrong road. In this scenario, your opinion does not coincide with the truth.

(2) You can be a blind man on the right road. What luck! This situation is not so bad. You can't know for sure that you are on the right road, but by chance you happen to be on it. In this scenario, your opinion happens to coincide with the truth.

(3) You can be a sighted man on the wrong road. This situation is not ideal but not terrible. At least you will be able to figure out eventually that you're on the wrong road. In this scenario, your

opinion is false, but at least you have the means to correct that opinion so it corresponds with the truth.

(4) You can be a sighted man on the right road. This is the ideal situation. You are on the right road, and you could prove it. In this scenario, you have a correct and provable opinion that corresponds with the truth.

Plato reasoned that the quest for knowledge resembles these scenarios. There are different opinions about the truth, but some are much more reliable than others because some actually correspond to provable facts.

The Four Types of Golfers

What does all this have to with improving our golf swings? Well, there are different types of golfers with different opinions about different ways to achieve the perfect swing. A Sophist would say that this variety of opinions means that there is no truth in the matter. The consequence of the relativist position is that we can never get a better swing because such a "better swing" does not exist objectively.

Plato would agree that there are different opinions about swings, *but some of these opinions are closer to the truth than others*. Let's examine the four types of golfers:

(1) There are terrible golfers with terrible swings who have no clue about the fundamentals and mechanics of the swing. They will never reach their destination: playing golf well.

(2) Then, there are golfers who have horrible technique; however, because they were lucky enough to be blessed with excellent coordination and athletic ability, they manage to play well despite the flaws in their technique. Very few golfers have this ability. They are blind, but happen to be on the right road. Good for them.

(3) Then, there are avid golfers who study the game but aren't that good. They have a clear knowledge about the mechanics of a sound swing, but they just can't put it into practice. Despite their excellent theoretical knowledge, it's difficult for them to reach their destination. However, since they have the correct knowledge, they are in a better position to reach their goals one day.

(4) Lastly, there are excellent golfers who not only study and understand the mechanics of a sound swing, but also put that knowledge to work on the course. They are on the right road, and they know why they are there. This is the ideal situation, because if they veer off course or if their swing breaks down, their theoretical knowledge helps them get back on track.

Becoming a better golfer requires a commitment to being one of the last two types of golfers. Plato, arguably the most influential philosopher in history, would insist that you really do have to learn and comprehend the fundamentals in order to become a better golfer. The fundamentals are grip, stance, posture, alignment, and aiming.

Golf Fundamental: The Grip

The grip is arguably the most important facet of the pre-swing or setup procedure. The grip is the only connection to the golf club that we have. To hold the club incorrectly or to hold it with the incorrect pressure will most likely lead to inconsistent and errant golf shots. It would be difficult to find good golfers today who do not use the "conventional" grip.

Take the time to analyze your grip. Are you holding the club in a conventional manner? As a right-handed golfer, the left hand needs to be placed on the grip in a slightly stronger position (angled to the right, crease between thumb and forefinger pointing towards the right shoulder) than the right hand. The right hand is in a more passive position on top on the left thumb with the crease between the thumb and forefinger pointing more vertically.

As a teacher, what I tend to see is the opposite of this. The left hand is in a weaker position than it should be (thumb too much on top and no knuckles in sight) and the right hand in an extremely strong position (the hand angled over to the right, thumb to the right side of the grip). This does feel strong, but can restrict the release of the club head and tends to get the club swinging from the outside in, causing a slice to the right for right-handed golfers. The correct grip is designed to allow maximum control with the left hand which in turn increases the ability to release the club head during the follow through.

Lastly, on the subject of grip pressure, many ideas and analogies have been written and discussed, but if we think of it on a scale of 1-10 (1 being the lightest grip and 10 a stranglehold) it should only be about a 4. There are few amateur golfers who hold the club too lightly!

Golf Fundamental: Stance

As you address the ball your feet should be shoulder width apart (or slightly wider) for a regular full shot and your knees should be slightly bent in an athletic position. Try to feel like a goalie waiting to save a penalty shot. You then bend over from the hips. Try not to curve your spine or roll your shoulders into a hunched position whilst doing this.

When teaching, I see many players who are either too hunched over or too erect. Having the chin up and not buried in their chest is also a vital element to the stance. I expect someone must have told them to keep their head down. And they do! This can restrict both the swing and the turn of the torso.

The main idea here is to have a straight spine, tilted at an angle, without feeling unnatural or forced. The ultimate goal is to maintain a constant spine angle throughout the entire swing.

Golf Fundamental: Posture

Posture is very closely linked to stance, and both relate to the setup of the body. The feet should be shoulder-width apart with the weight being slightly forward over the balls of the feet. The feet can be flared out slightly to help with the hip turn during the swing.

Posture is all about balance. The correct posture will allow for good dynamic balance from the ground up. All good swings come from the ground up. The rotation and coil that is used for power is only achieved if the player retains solid foundations from the ground and actually uses the ground as a pivot. Too many golfers lose the feeling of their feet on the ground and cannot use the terra firma as a springboard or launch pad for their swing.

The posture and stance that has been already been discussed must be athletic. The combination of stability and movement during the swing is vital. The swing is a flowing sequence and often a powerful combination of different movements. If our stance and posture are not dynamic and balanced, then it will be very difficult to maintain not just *our angles but also a steady head position during impact, which is a very important facet of the swing principles.*

As I noted, stance and posture are very closely linked and I think the best way to explain the differences between the two is that 1) stance is the more technical explanation of positions, i.e., where to place our feet, spine angle, knee flex, etc., prior to the swing starting, and 2) posture is the ability to maintain these angles during the swing. Good posture also prevents injury by maintaining balance throughout the swing process.

Good posture is defined as maintaining the primary and secondary curves and angles of the spine. Postural muscles give stability to the trunk area of the body so the golfer can pivot correctly to produce a smooth and efficient backswing and follow-through when playing golf.

The overweight golfer may find it difficult to rotate due to poor abdominal toning leading to poor posture at address. Also, a juvenile golfer's posture may be poor due to hitting an excessive number of practice balls, normally at full speed with his or her peers, with postural muscles that are not yet strong enough to cope with such a hard work load. This can lead to injury, poor posture and swing problems.

Also, posture may have to change depending on how the ball is lying. If the ball is below the player's feet, then the posture will have to change to allow for this by bending considerably more from the waist and spreading the feet a little wider than normal.

Golf Fundamental: Alignment

In the pre-swing setup we must be extremely aware of our aim and alignment. Don't be mistaken, these are very different! Alignment refers to the lining up of the feet, knees, hips, chest and shoulders at the address position prior to starting the swing.

When aligning your body, keep the clubface 90 degrees to the ball-to-target line and then settle into your stance. Make sure that while you are settling into your stance the clubface remains "square" to the target position.

When settling into your stance, you should have your toes, knees, hips, shoulders and eye line all parallel to the ball-to-target line. A useful image to remember is that of railway tracks, where the ball and club are on one track and your body is on the other track parallel left for right-handed golfers. These tracks should never meet and should be parallel to infinity.

If the angles close (both train tracks meet) then this is known as a closed alignment, which causes both pushed and pulled shots. Ideally we would like our arms to swing along the line our feet made at address; if these were facing to the right (closed for a right hander) then the swing path would become "in to out" and result in a push or sliced shot curving further to the right. However, golfers tend to sub-consciously know this and try to drag or pull the club and shot back on line. Tell-

tale signs of this happening are lack of balance on the forward swing and a shorter, even cut-off finish position. To check your alignment, put two clubs down on the ground: one club along the ball to target line and the other club along you toe line or behind your heels showing the alignment of your body—remember, the clubs should be parallel to infinity.

If we are hoping to hit the target more often, then this fundamental is one of the keys to our success. But remember, it is only the clubface that should point to the target; our feet, knees, hips, chest and shoulders should remain parallel left for a right handed player at setup.

Golf Fundamental: Aiming

Aiming refers to the direction the clubface is pointing in at the address position prior to the start of the swing. It does not refer to the aiming of the body as this is known as alignment and is covered in the previous section.

Aim is the direction the leading edge (bottom line) of the iron is pointing in at the address position. This should be straight at our target with the sole of the club flat on the turf. If the leading edge is misaligned left or right or the heel or toe of the club is too high, then the aiming of the clubface will be affected. Try placing a "Club Face Indicator" (which is a magnetic device that sticks on your clubface and shows *exactly where the clubface is pointed) onto the face of your iron. Then either move the leading edge open and closed or move your hands up and down. Just look how much the aim is affected by a small change in position!*

You should always begin your pre-shot routine by locating the target from BEHIND THE BALL. This is the only way you can clearly establish the target line you are aiming for.

Next you will select the line on which you plan to start the ball. Identify an intermediate target spot just a few feet in front of the ball. It could be a light blade of grass or a divot. Keep referring to this spot as you move into your stance from behind the ball. Aim the clubface first. Aim the clubface squarely at the intermediate target you selected earlier. Look up to check that your clubface, the spot, and your ultimate target are all in line. If they are, your aim is sound.

Conclusion

Plato is famous because he rejected the Sophists' powerful idea of relativism. Because of Plato, we can be confident that there are objective truths, despite the fact that people have different opinions about them. Because of Plato, we can be confident that we can achieve a better government by analyzing what makes governments good and bad.

Most importantly, because of Plato, we can also be confident that we can indeed become better golfers by analyzing what makes our swings good or bad. We can become better golfers by learning the truth of the matter, which is that the fundamentals are essential for all good golf swings.

So study golf, take lessons from a pro, and practice. There really is a right way to improve your game. Don't be a blind golfer in the woods. Be a sighted golfer in the fairway.

4 THE ARISTOTELIAN GOLFER

"If there is some object of activities that we do want for its own sake, and others only because of that…it is plain that this must be the good, the highest good. Would not knowing it have a great influence on our way of living?"

—Aristotle, *Nicomachean Ethics* (350 BC)

Why do we get out of bed in the morning? To work. Why do we work? To make money. Why do we make money? So we can play golf. Why, then, do we play golf? We either do so for its own sake or for another reason. If we golf for its own sake, then golfing is the highest good that we can achieve; it is the ultimate purpose of our existence. If we don't golf for its own sake, then why do we do it?

Questioning the purpose of things was a favorite pastime of ancient Greek philosophers. Why is the sky blue? Why does the rain fall? Why do plants grow? Why do animals exist? Why do humans exist? Why do we do what we do? Some philosophers attempted to create a system that would establish why all things exist. By doing so, they thought they could discover the meaning of life.

Aristotle

Aristotle (384-322 BC)—son of a royal physician, student of Plato, and tutor to the young prince of Macedonia who would later become Alexander the Great—believed he discovered what our ultimate purpose or our highest good is.

Aristotle was the first philosopher to address what things are and why they exist, and he developed a method for it. He asked the question "why?" persistently. Eventually, when he could not ask "why?" anymore, he believed he had discovered the ultimate purpose.

Aristotle believed that when we found our ultimate purpose, we would attain a state of being that he called *eudaimonia*, which is a difficult word to translate into English. It means happiness, but also contentment, satisfaction, vitality, and alertness, all in one. However, *eudaimonia* is not the simple pursuit of pleasure in the way animals might pursue it; it is more complex. Perhaps, it is something like the feeling you get when you are watching a high iron shot—which, when struck, feels absolutely perfect—floating gracefully towards the pin.

To live well for Aristotle is to achieve this state of *eudaimonia*. However, many of us fail to achieve it, because we do not know what our ultimate purpose is. We do not actually comprehend why we are doing what we are doing. We just go through the motions of our daily existence. We don't understand why we get up, work, earn money and play golf. With all of the difficulties in our lives, it is hard to grasp what we are really meant to be. Indeed, many people have wholly different answers to why they do what they do. Some see the big picture and others, the small.

Let's look at an example. If you were at a golf course under construction, you might ask a man in a truck delivering sod what he was doing. He might say, "I am delivering sod." However, if you were to ask a surveyor directing the sod dump, he might say, "I am creating a fairway." If you were then to ask the course architect what he was doing, he might say, "I am building a golf course."

The man delivering sod is not wrong for thinking that his purpose is limited to delivering sod exclusively; his conception of the project is limited. He cannot grasp the ultimate purpose.

Of course, one might then ask the architect why he is building the course. He might say because he needs to earn money. We might then ask why he needs to earn money. We could then continue to ask questions about why he does what he does until we arrive at an explanation that does not aim towards another goal, an "end-in-itself," or the ultimate purpose.

The Meaning of Life

So we get out of bed to work, which we do to make money, which we do so we can play golf. Why, then, do we play golf? To be happy. Why do we want to be happy?

Well, that's a silly question. We want to be happy because happiness is an "end-in-itself." There is nothing else for which happiness aims. The aim of work, money, and golf is eventually to make us happy, but happiness does not aim for something beyond itself. We do not wish to be happy in order to accomplish something else. Happiness is, therefore, the ultimate purpose and our highest good.

So how did Aristotle think we could succeed in actually living happy lives? We can do so in the same way we achieve success in golf. Aristotle suggests three methods: (1) selecting a target, (2) avoiding inferior goals, and (3) becoming well rounded.

Selecting a Target

First, we must have a target to aim at, the pin on the green. Just as poor aim destroys a golf shot, so failure to focus on our ultimate purpose prevents us from actually achieving the happiness we seek. Therefore, we must focus our minds continuously on that target, which is our highest good, a good for which nothing else aims—happiness. Having a target to aim at is, of course, crucial for golfers.

Golf Tip: Aim, Visualize, Commit

Lee Trevino once asked his caddy for the line of a shot while playing at the British Open at Royal Birkdale. The caddy suggested that he aim for a house on the horizon. Trevino said he knew the house was the line, but he wanted to know what window to aim at.

As you can see, with regard to target selection, pros have a much smaller target than amateurs. However, there is no reason why amateurs cannot learn to pick out small targets as well. Indeed, if you visualize every part of your shot before attempting it, your brain and your body are much more likely to execute that shot than if you just step up to the ball and whack it!

Sam Snead would often say that he would paint a picture in the sky of the shot he planned to hit. Jack Nicklaus would imagine the shape of the shot, the trajectory, and even how the ball would react when landing before he made his swing.

In order to sharpen your focus, try to visualize your shots. Stand behind the ball and visualize the shot you are about to play. The better you can picture the shot, the flight of the ball, and the result, the better chance you will have of actually executing it.

If in between clubs, be decisive and commit to the club of choice as well as the choice of shot. If you are unsure of the amount of break in a putt, again make a decision and commit to it. Once you have made up your mind, it is important to commit and pull the trigger!

Avoiding Inferior Goals

Second, we must be careful not to lose sight of that target by becoming distracted by inferior goals. Just like many amateur golfers concentrate on achieving greater distance, often at the expense of accuracy and consistency, so we are often distracted from our life's ultimate purpose by competing interests. For example, many think that the purpose of life is to make money, but Aristotle cautions us about this goal: "The life of money-making is in a sense a life of constraint, and it is clear that wealth is not the good we seek; for it is useful in a part as a means to something else." Remember that Aristotle asked the "why?" question until there was no other question to ask. Money is indeed useful, but only insofar as it helps us to achieve something else entirely—happiness. It is potentially a means to achieving the ultimate purpose, but it should not be valued as the ultimate purpose itself. Fame and power, similarly, are not valuable in and of themselves because these things aim at something else. Golfers too often set themselves inferior goals, but good golfers remember to focus on true goals.

Golf Tip: Eliminating Inferior Goals

Having goals is a great idea for improving our golf. But it is important that our goals are not only attainable but also realistic and measurable. Below is a great mnemonic for our golfing goals: SMARTER.

S - *specific*
M - *measured*
A - *attainable & adjustable*
R - *realistic*
T - *timed*
E - *enjoyable and exciting*
R - *recorded*

Most amateurs strive to hit the ball farther and spend hours on the range just smashing the driver as hard as possible, hoping to hit the ball farther and farther. However, without the correct grip, the release of the club head is not possible and the driver will probably keep slicing no matter how hard it is hit.

Also, I have noticed a great number of players go out on to the course and try to play each hole like a pro. They try to shoot par on as many holes as possible. This is an admirable but unfortunately unrealistic goal. Trying too hard and forcing the shots to make par only *result in frustration and bad shot after bad shot. Play to your handicap, work out where you get shots, and utilize those extra shots well. If you get a shot on a par 4, play conservatively. Instead of forcing the driver, hit a 3-wood or even an iron off the tee. Three well played shots will put the ball on the green. Who knows you may make the putt - PAR!*

Thinking you can hit that one-in-a-million shot will result in a disaster nearly a million times! Use your handicap to plot your way around the course and you will be less stressed and more positive—you will also score better. Remember, as Dr. Bob Rotella says, "This is not a game of perfect."

Becoming Well Rounded

Third, we must focus on becoming well rounded. Excellence on the golf course requires that players be well rounded. They must pay equal attention to every part of their game, from driving the ball accurately, to mastering the short game, to harnessing the power of their emotions. Sadly, most golfers not only skip short game practice, but they ignore the mental aspects of the game as well. Both of these oversights prevent many from excelling. For Aristotle, to excel at life meant to be well-rounded in all respects: to be a hard worker, but not a workaholic; to be educated, but not an egghead; to be physically fit, but not a health nut; to be spiritual, but not a God freak.

Golf Tip: The Aristotelian Golfer

As for Aristotle's writings on living a well-rounded life, this has a natural parallel in golf. As Dr. Sola says, we must pay equal attention to each and every part of our game, including the mental aspects.

As a teaching professional, I tend to see that most amateur golfers practice what they are good at. They practice shots that they feel confident they can execute repeatedly. They tend to shy away from weaker areas of their game. Surely, they should be doing just the opposite—working on the weakest parts of their game! Ideally, players should use whatever practice time they have to work on the parts of their game that they find the most challenging.

For example, the short game is undoubtedly a major part of this wonderful game, and a precise short game is an essential skill if you are hoping to play and score well. Structure your practice time so that a larger percentage is spent putting, chipping and pitching. If this part of your game is weaker, speak to a PGA professional and let him or her guide you through the fundamentals of the short game.

Also, bunker play can be thought of as one of the more difficult skills to master, but with the right instruction and practice, it can become a relatively simple shot to perform. Many tour players will intentionally aim for green side bunkers if the rough surrounding the green is extremely penal (at the US Open, for example) as good bunker players will feel that they are able to get much more control out of the bunker than from long grass. It is said that the great Gary Player spent up to six hours a day just on bunker shots! Imagine how confident he must have been if his ball did find a bunker whilst playing a round.

The final aspect of being well rounded, which is sometimes given only lip service, is the mental side of the game. It has been well documented that Tiger's father had US Special Forces shrinks speak with Tiger at a young age in an effort to improve his mental strength and focus. I am not expecting anyone to go to such lengths, but reading about and learning mental skills that will improve your focus—skills that are discussed in subsequent chapters—can only help you to become an even more well-rounded golfer.

In short, if we can become more well-rounded golfers by practicing all of the required skills needed on the course, we can come to the course much more confident and optimistic about performing well.

Conclusion

These three key ideas from Aristotle will hopefully lower your scores as well as improve your chances of achieving happiness. However, the most important idea is the first. Without having a target to aim at, we will fail on the course and in life. Having a target constantly before us not only greatly increases our chances of living a happy life, but it also improves our golf immeasurably.

Both life and golf are difficult games. It is easy to fail in both. Aristotle was keenly aware of the sadness and disappointment in many people's lives, but he wanted us to be happy. The greatest sadness for him was that many of us fail fully to achieve our ultimate purpose, either because we do not recognize it or because external obstacles prevent us from realizing it.

However, there is only one way to be a happy person and a scratch golfer—to aim consistently for happiness and nothing else. This is not easy. As Aristotle said, it is possible to fail in many ways, but it is only possible to succeed in one way.

In trying to live a happy life, failure is easy, but success is difficult.

In golf, missing your target is easy, but hitting your target is difficult.

In order to succeed in both life and golf, you must focus on your ultimate goals.

5 THE CYNICAL GOLFER

BERTRAND Russell, the great 20th century philosopher, suggests that there are four main types of philosophers. Some, the *comfortable philosophers*, are satisfied with the world in which they live. Their philosophy does not seek to change the status quo. Then there are the *reforming philosophers* who have some measure of confidence in the wisdom and intelligence of people in their society, so they concentrate on providing advice on how to improve the world in whatever ways they can, without completely tearing apart the social fabric. Others, the *revolutionary philosophers*, are wholly dissatisfied with the world. However, like reformers, they still have the confidence that philosophy has the power to radically alter society for the better. Still others, the *pessimistic philosophers*, have been dissatisfied with both the world and the people in it for so long that they become disillusioned and depressed. Not only do they despise what the world has become, but they also lack confidence in their ability to change it.

These four types of philosophers roughly correspond to four

types of golfers: *comfortable golfers*, those who are happy with their game; *reforming golfers*, those who seek to improve their game through slight improvements; *revolutionary golfers*, those who seek to improve through complete retooling of their swings; and *pessimistic golfers*, those who are so thoroughly disgusted with the game that they are on the verge of quitting. Most golfers probably resemble all of these types, at one time or another in their lives.

Today, we will look at the philosophical history of the last type, the wholly disgusted and disenchanted pessimists. Specifically, we'll look at the greatest of pessimists, the Cynics.

Antisthenes

The ideas that formed cynicism were first articulated by Antisthenes (c. 455-360 BC), a disciple of Socrates. Antisthenes was a wealthy Athenian aristocrat until the Athenian government condemned Socrates to death in 399 BC for corrupting the youth of Athens and for failing to worship the local gods. After this, Antisthenes became thoroughly disappointed with both the government of the city and the hypocrisy of civilized society.

Everything from fancy clothes to governments, he argued, only served to corrupt people. There was no escape but to return to a natural state. So Antisthenes renounced all of the comforts that his high social station provided him and took to teaching.

He created his own academy known as the Cynosarges, or the Silver Dog, where he lectured about the advantages of living a simple life, free of luxury.

Diogenes

Antisthenes' most famous student was Diogenes (c. 412-323 BC). Diogenes literally means the god-born (*dio* + *genes*), but his detractors called him the cynic (the dog) because he literally lived like a wild dog, with no home and no possessions. Indeed, the word *cynicism* comes from the Greek root *kyon* and the Latin *canus*, from which we derive the word *canine*.

Diogenes lived in a large jug, which some historians think was a wine barrel and others think was a ceramic pitcher used to bury the dead—a primitive coffin. He did briefly own a cup and a spoon, but he threw away the cup when he saw a boy drinking from his hands. "This child," he said, "has beaten me in simplicity." The spoon was discarded shortly thereafter when he saw another boy using a bread crust to eat soup.

Diogenes took Antisthenes' pessimism about society to the extreme. Everything that civilized human beings value is a counterfeit. Curiously, Diogenes' father was a counterfeiter. The great classical scholar Gilbert Murray describes Diogenes' project like this: "His aim in life was to do as his father had done, to 'deface the coinage,' but on a much larger scale. He would deface all the coinage current in the world. Every conventional stamp was false. The men stamped as generals and kings; the things stamped as honor and wisdom and happiness; all were base metal with lying superscription [with lies engraved on their faces]."

Diogenes broke all the rules, and I do mean all of them. In addition to masturbating in public, he lifted his leg, like a dog, on those who ridiculed him. He also walked around giving people the finger, pretending to be surprised when they took offense. In the winter, he hugged stone sculptures of men and women to remind himself that warmth and cold were merely physical sensations that could be overcome.

Diogenes believed in the happiness that comes with absolute liberty. This means living a life free from all physical urges and psychological desires, primarily the desire to feel accepted by society. Pain is the result of desires unfulfilled. If we can learn to eliminate all desires from our life, we will remove all of the causes of pain and unhappiness.

Eliminating Our Desires

The problem with civilization is that it encourages us to desire things which we don't really need. We want money. But money only makes us jealous and miserly. We want power. But power makes us corrupt and mean. We want prestige. But prestige makes us duplicitous and fake. We want style. But style is petty and childish.

Golfing culture is particularly susceptible to attacks by the Cynics. The more we try to fit in, the more opportunities there are for others to hurt us. We want that golf club membership so badly, but then we're not admitted and we're gutted. We want the powerful to recognize us, but they don't and we feel snubbed. Maybe if we buy that new Mercedes, we will get the prestige that we crave. Or maybe it's that new set of premium Callaways and a monogrammed golf bag. Diogenes, however, reminds us that the more we think we own our possessions, the more they begin to own us. The more status, power and wealth we attain, the less control we have.

Of course, golfing culture also has its own band of cynical dogs. John Daly is the Diogenes of the golf world. He is wholly incapable of fitting in, but he doesn't let it bother him. The fact that he is so *not-golf* is what makes him so popular. We admire the underdog, the black sheep, and the outsider because we sense the hypocrisy that exists behind the social niceties, civilized manners, and sheer elitism of golfing culture. We might have a subtle sense that if golf were wiped from the face of the Earth, it wouldn't really matter. And it wouldn't. We'd get on with our lives just fine. We'd find another pastime to entertain ourselves.

Indeed, when we begin to crave golf too much we are allowing golf to control our feelings more than we should, and the Cynics remind us that we should allow nothing to have such control over our happiness. Golf could be taken from us at any moment, as could our countries, families and homes.

Crates of Thebes, a disciple of Diogenes, did actually lose his country when it was conquered by Philip of Macedon. He was asked by the son of Philip, Alexander the Great (356-323 BC), if he would like his home returned to him. Crates replied, "What would be the use of it? Some other Alexander would come at some future time and destroy it again. But poverty and dear obscurity,/ Are what a prudent man should think his country;/ For these e'en fortune can't deprive him of."

So why don't we give up golf, our job and our possessions and just live our lives simply, like Diogenes? Well, very few people can be as pessimistic about the world as Diogenes, but we can still learn a lot from him. He reminds us that golf is just not that important. Nor is power, prestige or wealth.

Diogenes and Alexander

The most famous story about Diogenes involves his meeting with Alexander the Great in Corinth. Alexander's father, Philip, had united all of the independent Greek city states under his rule, and Corinth would witness the ceremony whereby Alexander would become the commanding general of the united Greek armies. The normal citizens prostrated themselves at the feet of the great prince and paid him homage. The wealthy and powerful flattered and complimented him, hoping for some imperial patronage.

Curiously, the most prominent philosopher in the city did not show to offer his congratulations. So, Alexander decided to find Diogenes in the jug that served as his home. He looked inside and asked if there was anything that he, the great prince, could do for the impoverished philosopher. Diogenes responded, "Just stand aside. You're blocking the light."

Alexander did not execute Diogenes for this affront to his dignity as many powerful princes would have done. Instead, he told his staff that if he were not Alexander, he would gladly be Diogenes.

Golf Tip: The Cynical Golfer

There is little that can be added here at least from a technical point of view; however, I do think certain aspects of Diogenes' philosophy can teach us a lot about our mental attitude during a difficult round of golf.

Most importantly, we must keep the game of golf in perspective. Each year, for the last ten years or so, I have been privileged to teach this wonderful game to a number of successful and influential medical doctors at one of the best golf course resorts in Europe, Val Do Lobo, Portugal. These men and women have worked tirelessly and professionally for many years diagnosing and treating adults and children, and then nursing them back to health. This is a vocation that I admire more than any other, and I feel a debt of gratitude is owed by the whole world to the skill and dedication of these medical professionals.

Yet, whilst on the range or on the course or even over dinner, each and every one of these men and women profess great admiration for my skill and achievements as a golfer. They feel that they too must master the game.

Now I do agree that playing this game well is a fantastic achievement and if someone can attain professional status and teach the game well, then that person should be very happy with what he or she has achieved. However, golf in no way compares to other professions, such as medicine, education and social service, which involve saving lives or making a difference in people's lives in other ways.

So, the next time you are on the course and your game starts to go somewhat awry, try to keep things in perspective. Take pride in what you do professionally and remember your blessings. Your spouse and children will still be there when you get home, your dog will still come to you wagging its tail, and I am sure you will still enjoy a healthy dinner to round off the day.

Having this slightly more cynical attitude will probably allow you to swing easier and with less tension, which I am sure will allow you to enjoy the game even more and not leave you with the daunting question of whether to quit or not!

Conclusion

Since none of us will rule the world like Alexander, it may be wise to cultivate some of the cynical thoughts of Diogenes. If we do, the next time we are snubbed on a golf outing, excluded from a golf club, offended by the arrogant fat-cat in our foursome, or ridiculed for not having the newest gear, we can swallow our pride, forget our vanity, and happily find both a better golf course to play at and also better company to play with.

Crates of Thebes reminds us:

'Tis not one town, nor one poor single house,

That is my country; but in every land

Each city and each dwelling seems to me,

A place for my reception ready made.

Even if some private clubs reject us, there are plenty of other courses that will welcome us with open arms. For the cynical golfer, any course can be your country, and every green your home.

6 THE HEDONISTIC GOLFER

"The proof that pleasure is the chief good is that we are from our childhood attracted to it without any deliberate choice of our own; and that when we have obtained it, we do not seek anything further, and also that there is nothing which we avoid so much as we do its opposite, which is pain."

—Diogenes Läertius,
Lives of Eminent Philosophers (c. 3rd Century AD)

WHAT are the most basic rights that we have? According to most political philosophers, they are life, liberty and the pursuit of happiness. If golfing makes you happy, then let no sourpuss stand between you and your happiness. Be a hedonist instead. The philosophy that tells us that it is our fundamental right to choose golf is hedonism, which comes from the Greek word for pleasure, *hedone*. Very simply, hedonism means that pleasure is good and pain is bad. Therefore, one should seek always to maximize pleasure and minimize pain.

So, on Saturday, when you should be running errands and doing chores, choose golf. On Sunday, when you feel guilty and think you ought to go to church because you didn't do your chores on Saturday, choose golf again. On Monday, when the boss wants you to attend yet another boring and pointless meeting, call in sick and choose golf yet again!

The number of forces that prevent us from choosing golf are too numerous to mention. Family, a guilty conscience, social expectations, parental obligations, the job—all these forces try to stand between us and golf. Ignore them. Choose golf.

After all, living in this world is difficult enough without people telling us what to do and making us feel guilty for not doing what they want us to. We only have one life, so we should ensure that life is as full of pleasure as possible. Always choose golf.

Hedonism

One of the primary goals of philosophy is to offer guidance about how we can achieve a happy life. We've already met some ancient Greek thinkers who thought we ought to choose virtue and duty over golf, but they were all sourpusses. Plato and Socrates argued that we achieve happiness by being good people and virtuous citizens, not by pursuing pleasure. Aristotle, one of the greatest sourpusses of all time, advocated temperance and moderation as the keys to happiness.

You, however, would rather play golf than read their long and boring lectures about how doing what you hate might eventually bring you happiness. As they drone on and on about how one day you *might attain happiness*, you'll be on the golf course every day *being happy*.

Hedonism arose in a time of instability and turmoil in the ancient Greek world. Many cities were losing their cherished independence. Wars, coups and slave rebellions were always a threat. The Greeks began to lose a sense of security; they lacked confidence in the future, so philosophers began to turn their attention away from the abstract thought of Plato and Aristotle. They turned their minds towards the question of how to achieve happiness in a difficult, chaotic and frightening world. As the distinguished Cambridge professor C.F. Angus suggested, "Philosophy [was] no longer the pillar of fire going before a few intrepid seekers after the truth: it [became] rather an ambulance following in the wake of the struggle for existence and picking up the weak and wounded." Philosophy, rather than being focused on creating better societies and creating more in-depth understandings of abstract truths, became focused on giving comfort to people who live in a world of pain, suffering and uncertainty.

Hedonism is the most simple philosophy to adopt when

living a life filled with uncertainty and insecurity. At any moment, your skull could be cracked by an out-of-control golf ball. Of course, you'll hear "Fore!" a split second later, as you breathe your last breath. Since life is uncertain—a golf ball, a drunk driver, a terrorist attack, a heart attack or a stroke could finish you off at any time—the hedonists suggest that you pursue pleasure as much as possible while you can.

Aristippus

The first great Hedonist philosopher was Aristippus (c. 430-350 BC). And he practiced what he preached. Once, when asked by a wealthy friend to choose the most beautiful of three courtesans to have for the night, Aristippus chose golf—he chose all three.

So why do we pursue pleasure anyway? Hedonists argue that this is a silly question. No one needs to wonder why. We don't ask why dogs like their bellies rubbed or why they like tasty treats. They just do. And we like pleasure too. We don't need to go to school to learn it. We don't need special training to achieve it. It's built into our natural being. Seeking pleasure is the single, most simple explanation for *everything* we do.

In fact, when we look at why people do what they do, it confirms this idea of the world. Everyone pursues what is most pleasurable. This view provides a simple and direct explanation of why anyone does anything. Mother Theresa devoted her life to helping the poor. She enjoyed it. It gave her pleasure. She was doing what made her happy. To think she was a saint for doing what she did misses the point. She did it because it made her happy.

Hedonists argue that it's senseless to say that you and I should strive to live like her. We should not strive to be "good" and "moral" and give up everything to help the poor if doing so doesn't give us pleasure. After all, we all determine our own kinds of pleasure and they are all different. Mother Theresa chose charity; you may choose golf. We live how we live and that is how we think we can maximize our pleasure. There is no objective standard of pleasure. For everyone it's different.

Furthermore, there's no right and wrong and certainly no such thing as morality because:

Good = that which gives us pleasure

and

Evil = that which causes us pain

If everyone is doing what gives them pleasure, who's to say that there is an objective standard of right and wrong?

It's sad to say that, when faced with a choice, we often don't choose golf. So why don't we always do what is pleasurable? Hedonists suggest that we are shamed into not doing it by forces that tell us we have other duties and obligations besides pleasure. This is what makes us unhappy. It's best to abandon what society thinks, and do what is natural. Some people, like Mother Theresa, happen to enjoy how society wants us to behave. If you enjoy being a good parent or a charitable person, then do it! However, if you don't enjoy it, don't feel guilty about not doing it.

Guilt is not a source of pleasure, so Aristippus argues that it would be best to get rid of it. Guilt arises from a society that wants us to limit our pleasures. This is unnatural. Far better to pursue pleasure without shame, guilt or second thoughts.

Furthermore, Aristippus argues that we shouldn't feel guilty for playing golf on Saturday instead of, say, being a "responsible" parent and taking our kids to Play Land or watching their torturous choir rehearsal. When asked about why he abandoned his own son, Aristippus replied, "I know that phlegm, and I know that lice, proceed from us, but still we cast them away as useless."

Aristippus wasn't necessarily a nice guy, but at least he stuck to his guns. Who cares about being nice anyway if it doesn't make us happy?

Golf Tip: The Hedonist Golfer

We all want to enjoy our rounds, but sometimes no matter how much we are looking forward to it, it may start badly. Before we know it, we can't wait to get off the course and back home again! We should really be enjoying the round, because it's been a long and tiresome week. This is our time to play golf in nice company and in beautiful surroundings.

So how do we do make sure we can be good hedonists and enjoy our rounds, no matter what happens?

Firstly, we must put things in perspective. How much coaching have we had? How much practice have we been able to do? If the answer to both of these questions is "minimal," then going out and playing really well is probably not going to happen. This we must accept. With the best will in the world, hitting every shot well for over four hours is maybe asking just too much.

A lot of the problem is expectation. I am sure you have had a time in your life where you have not been able to play golf for quite some time. Your first 18 holes eventually arrives, so without any expectations you go out and play nice golf and score well. However, the next few times you are out, the expectations are naturally higher, and suddenly you can't hit a barn door with a banjo! It's all about expectation and attitude. After not playing for a while, you are not expecting to play well; you relax and swing and before you know it the game is over; you have scored well and everyone is happy. Once our expectations rise, we tend to try a little too hard, forcing the shots and focusing more on the outcome than the shot in hand. This leads to another bad day at the office.

Secondly, it is important to try to remain positive during the round. Keeping a positive and happy demeanor whilst the golfing gods are throwing their worst at you will not only give you a better opportunity of continuing your round without imploding, but it will also ensure you remain good company for your playing partners and, more importantly, enjoy your own game like a good Hedonist tells you to.

Some people, even pros, find enjoying this game much more difficult than others. Look at one of Europe's best-ever golfers, Colin Montgomery. Over the years he has let bad breaks, heckling from spectators and cars backfiring from 300 miles away affect his subsequent shots. There is no doubt that Montgomery had not only the talent to win a major, but also a game that was made for winning majors, and yet to date that particular honor has yet to be achieved. Off the course Montgomery is very humorous, and yet on the course his demeanor tends to change and the smallest irritations or mistakes magnify themselves into serious issues.

At a major event in the States some time ago, Montgomery's first name was announced as "Coe-lin" (as in Colin Powell), an innocent mistake from the starter at which many golfers would not have batted an eye-lid. However, Montgomery felt the need to correct the starter there and then with a look that could have sunk the Queen Elizabeth II. I am sure his inability to control his reactions had some effect on his next few shots.

Montgomery is an absolute genius when it comes to ball striking. He won the European order of merit some seven years in succession. Therefore, it can be assumed that the only thing that has stopped this exceptional golfer from winning more tournaments is his struggle with controlling his attitude and demeanor on the golf course.

Remaining positive and calm whilst playing a round is sometimes much harder than it should be. But by including in your game some of the tips mentioned in this book, there is no reason why your attitude and demeanor cannot improve, giving you a much more positive perspective and outlook for the remaining holes.

Golf Tip: Preparing for Pressure

One specific way to become a hedonist golfer is to learn to enjoy the pleasure of pressure situations. Getting used to hitting shots under pressure will help you to perform well under pressure and will ultimately help you to succeed. There are many drills to help with this.

For putting pressure simulation, set out 3 balls from a hole on the putting green at 1-foot gaps and then repeat this around the hole in 2- and 3-foot gaps. Now begin by knocking in all the 1-foot putts, then go on to the 2-footers and then the 3-footers. However, if you miss one putt, you must start over again! The pressure will build as you near the end because you won't want to start all over again.

For driving pressure simulation, imagine the parameters of a fairway on the range and tee off with 10 balls one after the other. See how many stay within the parameters and record your best score. Play again, and try to beat your best score. As you continue the game and improve, the pressure will build as you try to beat your personal best.

Conclusion

Hedonism has some distinct advantages over other ways of living. Most importantly, it makes one independent from all of the chances and uncertainties that wreck our days and ruin our plans. "If all the laws are eliminated," Aristippus said, "we hedonists should still live in the same manner as we do now." If our one goal is to maximize pleasure, it doesn't matter if we live in a dictatorship or a democracy, in the third world or the first, as a millionaire or a slave. Diogenes Läertius (not to be confused with Diogenes, the Cynic) described this view as follows: "Wealth and poverty have no influence at all on pleasure, for rich men are not affected by pleasure in a different manner from poor men. In the same way…slavery and freedom are things indifferent, if measured by the standard of pleasure, and nobility and baseness of birth, and glory and infamy."

Furthermore, hedonism teaches us what to value. Things are useful only insofar as they give us pleasure. Take money for instance. Many people value money, but Aristippus cautions us about that value. Money is not important in itself, it's only important as a means to an end—it is only useful if it can somehow give us pleasure. Once on a sailing ship about to be attacked by pirates, Aristippus threw all of his gold coins in the sea, arguing that "it was better for the money to be lost for the sake of Aristippus, than Aristippus for the sake of his money."

So, the next time you face a difficult decision in life about doing what you should do versus what would make you happy, remember the hedonists—and always choose golf.

7 THE EPICUREAN GOLFER

AS we continue our quest to achieve happiness on the golf course and in life, we remember that in the last column we met Aristippus, the hedonist. Hedonism is an uncomplicated way of life. It describes the reason why we live—to maximize our pleasure. It organizes everything that affects our lives into two simple categories of pleasure and pain, and then commands us to always choose pleasure. Hedonists tell us to choose golf. They argue that if we always golf when we want to, we will live happier lives.

However, some hedonist thinkers who followed Aristippus suggested that having too much fun was not a good thing. They agreed with hedonists about pleasure being the root of happiness, but they had different ways of achieving it—through prudence and moderation.

Epicurus

"The greatest good of all is prudence:
it is a more precious thing than even philosophy."

In this chapter, we continue on the theme of happiness, but in a more sophisticated way. Today, you will meet Epicurus (341-270 BC), who accepted pleasure as the meaning of life, but rejected the simple hedonist understanding of pleasure.

Epicurus was an expatriate Athenian living in Samos, an island on the eastern edge of the Aegean sea, next to what is now Turkey. The early part of his life was not stable, which might account for his philosophical views about moderation and simplicity. He was poor. When he was eighteen, his family, as well as all Athenians, were expelled from Samos. They were forced to become refugees. Eventually, he was able to study philosophy and founded his own school on the island of Lesbos, before returning to Athens in 307, when he was about thirty-four.

In Athens he established what we would now think of as a commune. Everyone was welcome, including women, children, slaves and prostitutes—a revolutionary policy for the status-conscious Athenians. His home was a golf club in which anyone could be a member. His philosophy of happiness was truly one that was meant to embrace people of all classes. This is a remarkable departure from some of the previous philosophies we have seen, which have pretty much ignored the existence of everyone except educated, male citizens with both social status and wealth. For example, Aristotle, who was famously dismissive of slaves, wrote in *Politics*, "Some men are by nature free, and others slaves, and for the latter slavery is both expedient and right."

Much of the earlier abstract philosophy of the ancient world would have been limited to those with the resources to obtain an education, which is sadly no different than it is today. Indeed, the practice of golf and the study of philosophy are too often limited to certain socioeconomic classes. This reminds us that we should, like Epicurus, do all we can to broaden access to both the golf course and the classroom.

Revising Hedonism

In addition to making the revolutionary decision to open his home to all people, Epicurus revolutionized the pursuit of pleasure by making some important additions to simple hedonism. Hedonists were not necessarily philosophical. However, Epicurus was. He believed that the role of philosophy was to teach people how to become happy. All other goals of philosophy—the discovery of the nature of truth, the clarification of abstractions, the study of the natural world—were bankrupt. He insisted, "Vain is the word of a philosopher which does not heal any suffering of man. For just as there is no profit in medicine if it does not expel diseases of the body, so there is no profit in philosophy if it does not expel the suffering of the mind."

In an effort to heal our suffering, Epicurus first identifies the things that cause us pain; doing so will prepare the way for more pleasure.

The first cause of pain is physical. Physical pain is something that we all have to deal with eventually, so Epicurus advises that all people must be trained to endure pain. One way of doing so was, contrary to the hedonist view, to avoid unnecessary pleasure. For example, if you are accustomed to fine foods and wines, if those are taken away, it leads to disappointment.

However, if you are accustomed to simple foods, your hunger will be satisfied and you will never cry over the loss of a juicy steak. It is curious that to be an "Epicurean" today means that you enjoy fine dining and gourmet food. This is not what Epicurus advocated. His own diet was simple, and he preferred bread and water to delicacies. Only at festivals would he indulge in a little cheese. We should also heed Epicurus' insistence on the careful selection of luxuries. When we become accustomed to golfing too much, it may cause us pain when we cannot play.

The second cause of pain is mental. In other words, false ideas or incorrect beliefs cause us pain, and Epicurus identifies two that cause pain: a belief in the supernatural and the fear of death. If we can only eliminate those ideas, we will be happy. For many people, the belief in Hell prevents us from pursuing pleasure as much as we should, because we don't want to suffer for all eternity because we pursued pleasure on Earth.

Also, many of us fear death. Epicurus reminds us that we ought not to fear something that we cannot feel. Indeed, when we're dead, we won't feel anything. Epicurus writes, "All good and evil lies in sensation and sensation ends with death." So why fear something we won't feel? "Death, the most dreaded of evils," he says, "is therefore of no concern to us; for while we exist death is not present, and when death is present we no longer exist."

Maximizing Pleasure

Epicurus suggests that we can achieve happiness by managing our pleasure in such a way as to avoid pain—through understanding what social expectations have the power to upset us and what physical things we truly need and what are merely desires.

He writes, "To be accustomed to simple and plain living is conducive to health and makes a man ready for the necessary tasks of life. It also makes us more ready for the enjoyment of luxury, if at intervals we chance to meet with it, and it makes us fearless against the future." In this respect, he reminds us of

Aristotle, who advocated moderation in all things as the way to achieve happiness.

In other respects, Epicurus reminds us of the Cynics in his rejection of social expectations. There are many things that we value for the sake of our vanity. These are luxuries like a fancy car, a nice set of clubs, a prestigious golf membership, etc. Epicurus reminds us that we can be perfectly happy without them. We could, after all, drive a junker to the municipal course, rent a rotten set of clubs, and still shoot well enough to enjoy a round with our friends.

There are other things we value because they are natural, instinctual desires. Sex, for instance, is a natural desire. However, we don't need to have sex all the time in order to be happy. Epicurus recommends controlling that desire, so we are not pained when we can't have it. Eating is another natural desire, but we know that if we ate all the time then we would probably be worse off in the long run.

There are, then, true necessities that we must have in order to live well. Food is a necessity, as are water, clothing and shelter. Without these, we are indeed not living well.

However, there are other things that simply make our life easier, but we can dispense with them. We need chairs to sit on and desks to do work at. However, we don't need the most expensive chair or the most expensive desk. In golf, we don't necessarily need the most up-to-date equipment in order to excel. A pro could probably score very well with old equipment. New clubs only make golfing easier, but they are not required to be happy on the course.

Lastly, there are those things that are necessary to achieve human happiness, of which there was only one for Epicurus: friendship. All humans seek friendship, and Epicurus suggests it is impossible to be happy without it. Crucially, friendship is open to all of us, regardless of our wealth or status. A slave, a king, the rich and poor, the sick and healthy all crave friendship, which is the greatest happiness we can have.

Both hedonists and Epicurus agree that pleasure is the root of all happiness, but they disagree on how to understand pleasure. Hedonists suggest that we maximize the quantity of our pleasure, but Epicurus insists that we maximize the quality instead.

Golf Tip: The Epicurean Golfer

Epicurus tells us to avoid pain and maximize the quality of our pleasure, and the best way to do this is to learn how to recover from bad shots. The key is to plan for but not to expect perfect shots. After all, a bad shot can lead to a good one, and dwelling on the bad shot only causes unnecessary pain.

Think about your mental attitude during a round. Does one mistake cause you to unravel? Some players expect that anything less than a flawless round is a failure. But if you expect too much of yourself, you are setting yourself up for certain frustration. No one can be perfect. You must learn to accept that you are human and humans make mistakes. Allow yourself the luxury of making mistakes by giving yourself permission to make mistakes before the round begins. Even the best players in the world on top of their game make mistakes. You must accept mistakes so you can stay calm and composed.

The best players in the world hit bad shots, and you will hit bad shots as well. It's how we deal with those shots that counts. The better players do not try to make up the distance they may have just lost from the bad shot; instead, they re-focus and try to hit the best shot they possibly can. They accept that the previous shot happened and forget it.

Even the best players in the world handle errant or bad shots differently. Look at Freddy Couples or Jason Dufner. If you were not to see the result of their shots, it would be impossible to know whether the shot was perfect or terrible. Their demeanor does not change and their attitude remains constant. On the other side of the scale are players like Craig Stadler, who wear their hearts on their sleeves a little more and can sometimes allow the frustrations of this game to manifest themselves for all to see. Still, it is no coincidence that the players who have learnt to control their emotions better are the most successful in the game.

I have been extremely honored to have worked for Tiger for some time, and one of the many things that I have been impressed with is his ability to "move on" from bad shots. Early on in his career he had the 10-step rule, which meant that no matter how bad the shot was or how disappointed he was by a shot, once he had walked the 10 paces forward, it was gone—100 percent gone. Now was the time to begin thinking about the next shot and the next strategy. Try to adopt a similar rule in order to help yourself along the recovery process.

As mentioned in the Parmenides section, having a pre-shot routine and sticking to it is a great way to ensure that after a bad shot you do not rush the next shot you are about to play. Rushing into the next shot, still angry at the previous shot, is a sure way of compounding the error. Pre-shot routines give us the chance to calm down, re-focus and concentrate 100 percent on the shot in hand.

So remember Epicurus' teachings. You will learn to expect bad shots in your round, and when they occur you will also be ready to move on. When you move on, you will be able to enjoy the pleasure this beautiful game provides even more.

Conclusion

So how can we maximize the quality of our pleasure both in life and on the golf course?

Epicurus would suggest that we need to manage our rounds like we manage our lives. Indeed, our lives resemble a round of golf. Each day is a shot, each shot an opportunity to experience pain or pleasure. Sadly, as Blue reminds us, we often allow bad shots to ruin the next shot, just like we allow a bad day to ruin the next. When we let a bad shot affect the next shot and the next and the next until we've ruined our entire round, it is like allowing one bad day to affect an entire year.

Everyone knows that a round comes with both great shots and terrible ones, pleasure and pain, good luck and bad. Epicurus tells us that by being prepared to accept the pain, we will be better prepared for the pleasure when it comes. This will not only minimize the extent of the pain, but also increase the intensity of the pleasure.

So do not let one bad shot affect the opportunities that are possible in the next shot. Train your mind to minimize the mental pain a poor hit causes. At the same time, train your mind to maximize the pleasure that a good strike provides.

After all, golf like life comes with both the good and the bad, pleasure and pain. Golf is supposed to be fun, a source of pleasure, so don't let it become a source of pain. All intelligent golfers know, like Epicurus, that they must accept the pain when it happens, because an opportunity for pleasure is waiting on the next tee.

8 THE STOIC GOLFER

"Begin the morning by saying to thyself, I shall meet with the busy-body, the ungrateful, arrogant, deceitful, envious, unsocial..."

—Marcus Aurelius,
Meditations (2nd century AD)

MARCUS Aurelius certainly had a depressing morning routine. As the Emperor of Rome, he was probably the most powerful man in the world, but still he felt it necessary to prepare for his day with a dose of pessimism that one would more likely hear from a caddy, a cubicle worker or a customer service representative—not from the ruler of a vast empire stretching from the British Isles to the Arabian Peninsula.

This was his daily advice to himself as emperor, but if given the opportunity, he would also remind you the next time you play golf to begin *thy* round by telling *thyself*: "Today, my foursome will be full of arrogant and deceitful cheats. My round will be full of bad kicks, missed putts, plugged lies and muddy balls. My golf cart will break down on the 14th hole. My friend will intentionally belch on the backswing of my birdie putt. The group in front of me will be unbelievably slow, and the ranger will accuse *me* of not keeping pace. A renegade squirrel will steal my sandwich—and I will lose."

If you tell yourself this, you will be more powerful than Marcus Aurelius himself. You will command the universe, not just a large chunk of the Earth. You will be a Stoic.

Upon first glance, you might think this stoical approach to your day will be negative and pessimistic—a recipe for a disastrous performance on the course and a depressing day of life. However, upon careful inspection, Stoicism ought to be seen as sensible, mature, positive and even life-affirming.

This is what the Stoics believe. We constantly attempt to control aspects of our life that we have no control over. But why do we think we can control things that we know deep down are uncontrollable? When bad stuff happens, we whine and complain and whine some more. The Stoics remind us that when we complain and whine, *we are causing ourselves misery* because we can't let go of our sense of control.

While you're in mid-swing, your playing companion coughs, and you send your drive OB. Internally, you are fuming, but you keep it to yourself. You tee off again, but the tension from the previous distraction lingers, and you hit a mediocre shot that will play, but you're sitting three. Of course, your companion hits a boomer up the gut. "Oh, the injustice of it all! Why me?"

A Stoic would tell you to stop whining and get on with your round.

Zeno of Citium

Stoicism originated in ancient Greece in the fourth century BC. Its founder, Zeno of Citium, was born in Cyprus but moved to Athens in his youth. While in Athens Zeno was profoundly influenced by the pre-Socratics as well as Socrates, Plato and Diogenes (all of whom we met in previous chapters). From the pre-Socratics, he learned to study natural philosophy; from Socrates, to prize the virtuous life; from Plato, to understand and accept the order and reason of the universe; and from Diogenes, to remember that the desire for power, status and wealth leads to unhappiness.

From this patchwork of influences, Zeno developed the three central ideas of Stoicism, all of which are intended to help us live lives full of peace and happiness: first, we should give up trying to control things beyond our control; second, unhappiness is caused by our inability to accept our lack of control; and third, we should only try to control what is in our control, namely our own mental attitude. These ideas are particularly useful for golfers to remember while on the course.

Golf Tip: The Three-Hole Game

Zeno believes that frustration is easier to handle if you understand why it exists. Frustration can be caused by not getting what you want when you want it. You then become impatient and angry. You can reduce your frustrations by focusing on what you can achieve and then by building on your successes, instead of dwelling on your failures or frustrations. You cannot always control the outcome of a round, but you can always control your mental attitude.

A round of golf is long and grueling. Eighteen holes, each with its own special dangers, must be managed. For many players, however, one bad hole can ruin a day of seventeen good ones. Golfing well requires both mental and physical stamina, but it is precisely their mental strength that most amateur golfers neglect. One critical part of mental strength is not allowing one bad hole to ruin your day.

One of the ways you can control your emotions is to split the round into three-hole segments. Allow yourself a handicap for those three holes before playing them. For example, if you are an eighteen-handicapper you would allow yourself three shots over par for each three-hole segment. You play the first of the three holes two over, but you do not get anxious or frustrated because you are still on track. You par the second hole, so you're still okay. Whether you par or bogey the final hole of the first three, you have managed to play the holes without the frustration and anxiety you would normally have had because you have remained patient and managed your expectations.

You can also modify the game. For example, if you score a quadruple bogey on the second hole, then the run of three holes would stop and the third hole would become the first of the next three-hole segment. Doing this, you will force yourself to forget about the bad hole, and your mind will be refreshed with a new goal and a new game plan.

The Three-Hole Game will teach you how to stay focused, calm and in control over shorter periods of time. It will also teach you how to recover mentally from a bad hole. After a while, you will develop mental stamina that will last the whole eighteen.

The Stoic *Logos*

"Everything harmonizes with me, which is harmonious to thee, O Universe. Nothing for me is too early nor too late, which is in due time for thee. Everything is fruit to me which thy seasons bring, O Nature: from thee are all things, in thee are all things, to thee all things return."

—Marcus Aurelius, *Meditations*

We have seen that there are two dominant themes that appear

throughout the history of philosophy: the study of the universe and the study of humanity. Natural philosophers like Heraclitus and Parmenides concentrated on understanding the physical world, while philosophers like Socrates and Diogenes focused on developing human virtue. Some intrepid philosophers, however, tried to join the two main areas of study in grand schemes that attempted to explain both nature and man together. Plato's theory of knowledge was one system that attempted to show that the reason of the universe was comprehendible by the reasoning capacity of the human mind. Humans could create a good government and a good society by obeying the universal laws of reason. Aristotle also tried to connect the natural world to the human being through his notion of *telos*. All things in nature, including human beings, have a purpose, which is to reach their full development as what they fundamentally are. The Christian theologians, whom we will meet in the next chapter, also tried to synthesize these two themes. They developed the notion of a perfect God who created both nature and human beings. God gave human beings the gift of reason, which we should use in order to understand the perfection of His universe and in order to help with the perfection of our own souls.

The Stoics also attempted to create a system that joined the natural universe to human beings, and they did this through the concept of *logos* (from which we have derived the term *logic* and the suffix *logy* for the study of something). It is difficult to define *logos*, since it has numerous translations, but it means something like Reason, Truth, Order, Logic, God, Providence, Nature, and the Universe, all in one. The Stoics believed that *logos* made the universe an orderly and rational place—in fact, *logos* is the universe. And we humans are a part of that *logos*, so we are *logos* as well. We are connected to *logos* through both our physical existence and through our souls. However, only our souls are eternal; our bodies will eventually pass into dust. Some Stoics conceived of *logos* as the Eternal Fire which shoots off the sparks that become our minds and souls. These undying sparks will return to the Eternal Fire when our short physical lives end.

The concept of *logos* allowed the Stoics to develop a conception of the world in which they never felt troubled, frustrated or angry. Everything happens for a reason. It is not our place to complain about good or bad fortune. As Marcus Aurelius said:

> Constantly regard the universe as one living being, having one substance and one soul; and observe how all things have reference to one perception, the perception of this one living being; and how all things act with one movement; and how all things are the co-operating causes of all things which exist....

This is the notion of *logos*, from which many have drawn comfort when facing challenges in life and on the course. Since everything is *one*, bound in *logos*, we need to stop thinking of the world as something that punishes or annoys us. Instead, we should understand and truly believe that everything happens for a reason.

One important consequence of this belief in *logos* is that it forces us to become more respectful of others. We have already seen that Marcus Aurelius prepared himself every day for his inevitable encounters with the arrogant and deceitful, but here is the remainder of his morning memo:

> All these things happen to them by reason of their ignorance of what is good and evil. But I who have seen the nature of the good that it is beautiful, and of the bad that it is ugly, and the nature of him who does wrong, that it is akin to me, not only of the same blood or seed, but that it participates in the same intelligence and the same portion of the divinity, I can neither be injured by any of them, for no one can fix on me what is ugly, nor can I be angry with my kinsman, nor hate him, for we are made for co-operation, like feet, like hands, like eyelids, like the rows of the upper and lower teeth. To act against one another then is contrary to nature; and it is acting against one another to be vexed and to turn away.

Marcus Aurelius reminds us that we should respect others, despite their flaws, because we are all fellow citizens of the universe and fellow golfers. We all participate in *logos*. We are all one.

*

Golf Tip: Love the Logos

We live our lives with others, and we play golf with others too. Conflict is inevitable. Of course, you know that you cannot control how other players play or what they do. But how many times have you been irritated by the good breaks your friends get compared to yet another bad break for you? How many times have you been frustrated because your friend cheated and won a hole, but denied it when confronted? How many times have you let things outside of your control wreck your game?

We cannot directly affect the scores that our playing partners are producing, and yet we sometimes find ourselves more interested in their scores, their shots, and their decisions than in our own. So, learn to embrace your playing partners' good luck. Hope that they play well. Hope for a close match with lots of pressure shots. This attitude will ensure your mental state remains positive and calm. You will also stay focused on your own game and less on theirs.

We have all at some time been guilty of wishing ill on our opponents (in a nice way, of course) and, after all, we do want to win, but golf is a game of honor and respect, so let's focus on the good golfing logos *and, who knows, maybe the golfing gods will smile down on us for a change!*

Epictetus

"If you wish your children, and your wife, and your friends to live forever, you are stupid; for you wish to be in control of things which you cannot…."

—Epictetus,
Enchiridion (135 A. D.)

A stoic would have little sympathy for those who bemoan their bad fortune in life or on the course. After all, when you were born, who told you that you would be the only person in history who would never be fooled, rejected, harmed, insulted, or ridiculed, the only person to never experience sadness, grief, fear and hopelessness? The Stoics take this idea even further. The most rigorous, unapologetic and grumpy Stoic was Epictetus (c. 51-135 AD), who spent much of his life being tortured by various masters including Epaphroditus, an advisor to the evil fiddler Nero.

Epictetus grumbles: "I must die, but must I die groaning? I must be imprisoned, but must I whine as well?" If an evil dictator were to threaten to chop off your head, Epictetus suggests that you accept it with good humor. After all, you should tell him, "Do as you will. When did I ever tell you that I was the only man in the world who was exempt from beheading?"

And so, when you decide to play golf, remind yourself about what often happens when you golf. In other words, be mentally prepared for the disappointment and frustration that often accompanies golf.

When going to bathe at the Roman baths, Epictetus gave the following advice: "Picture to yourself the things which usually happen in the bath: some people splash the water, some push, some use abusive language, and others steal." When embarking on a round of golf, remind yourself that the group ahead will be slow, the company will be less than ideal, a rain storm will end your day early—and you will lose.

Without a doubt, Epictetus' experience as a slave made the Stoic philosophy more agreeable to him. He was often the victim of torture. One master tortured him for a mistake that another slave had made. His leg was bound in a rack and twisted until it snapped, an injury that caused great pain until the day he died.

Despite his difficult life, he always maintained his sense of calm and mastery over his own fate. Eventually, Epictetus became a free man and a famous teacher. His *Enchiridion*, a handbook of his philosophical views, became the manual for the Roman legions. His trials were not over, however. The Emperor Domitian banished him, along with all philosophers, from Rome, a decree that forced Epictetus to live in exile until the day he died.

Marcus Aurelius

"Thou art but a little soul bearing about a corpse."

—Marcus Aurelius,
attributed to Epictetus, *Meditations*

As Epictetus, the slave, approached the end of his life, the second great Roman Stoic, the Emperor Marcus Aurelius (121-180 AD), was beginning his. It is important to note that Stoicism is intended for all of us, emperors and plebeians, masters and slaves, players and caddies. (Yes, caddies of the world, as terrible as your master is, at least he won't torture you if you can't find his ball in the fescue.)

Marcus Aurelius, one of the few great and virtuous Roman emperors, lived his life according to the Stoic ideals of self-sufficiency and self-control. At the age of twelve, he adopted the Stoic philosophy, to which he committed his life. Loved by his subjects, the great emperor suffered endless trials protecting them and their empire. He lost four of his five sons, overcame acts of treason by his generals, and coped with the alleged adulterous behavior of his wife. Faced with challenges on the borders of the empire, he spent much of his reign far from the comforts of Rome, waging military campaigns against barbarians and penning his great contribution to philosophy, the *Meditations*. Edward

Gibbon, the famous eighteenth century Roman historian, praised Marcus Aurelius for being "severe to himself, indulgent to the imperfections of others, just and beneficent to all mankind." He was adored by the Romans long after his death, which occurred while waging war against the barbarians in what is now Austria.

Aside from reminding himself every morning about how many different varieties of jerks he would meet that particular day, Marcus Aurelius always asserted that the Stoic must learn to live *within* himself:

> Men seek retreats for themselves, houses in the country, seashores, and mountains...But this is altogether a mark of the most common sort of men, for it is in thy power whenever thou shalt choose to retire into thyself. For nowhere either with more quiet or more freedom from trouble does a man retire than into his own soul...and I affirm that tranquility is nothing else than the good ordering of the mind.

Caution aspiring retirees! It is not retiring to Florida and securing a coveted club membership that will bring happiness, but the condition of one's own mind. The well-ordered mind represents the limit of our control over the world; it, alone, is what we should train and develop. No one else causes our own unhappiness. We cause it based on irrational ideas about the world. Even though he was the most powerful man in the world, Marcus Aurelius tried his entire life to resign himself to his fate, whatever that might be.

Golf Tip: The Well-Ordered Golfing Mind

There are many techniques that can be used to reduce your frustrations and achieve the Stoic ideal of a well-ordered mind. Two relaxation techniques—breathing exercises and good visualization techniques—are widely used on both the PGA and European Tours. First, always make sure you start your pre-shot routine with a couple of deep breaths in order to focus your mind and relax your body. Second, always imagine the shot you want to hit before you hit it. Be positive. Picture a shot similar to one you played successfully in the past to bring about this positive imagery.

Positive self-talk is another common method of reducing both anxiety and frustration, which in turn will fill your mind with positive images. Talk to yourself. Talk to the ball. Tell the ball what it should do, and the ball will probably do it. This is extremely common place amongst the top players in the world and once you master the process, your golf will improve and your scores will plummet.

Try these techniques and they will relieve a lot of frustration during your round, especially if you are honest with yourself and acknowledge your present limitations. As you gain more control over yourself and improve the process, you will become less frustrated and more confident in your ability to succeed. You will have a well-ordered mind.

Stoic Resignation

Both Aurelius and Epictetus advocated a form of resignation to what the universe provides us, good or bad. The most extreme version of stoic resignation involves how we view our own relationships. If a friend complains about breaking his favorite driver, we don't allow it to affect our game. However, if we break our own favorite driver, we allow it to affect us. Epictetus cannot understand why we don't react the same way to both situations. He tells us to transfer our reaction about our friend's driver to our own in order to maintain our tranquility.

He even insists we transfer this concept to more important matters than broken drivers: "Someone else's child is dead, or his wife. There is no one who would not say, 'It's the lot of a human being [for loved ones to die].' But when one's own die, immediately it is, 'Alas! Poor me!'" Reminding ourselves that we are not special helps us maintain a calm and orderly mind.

Once we develop a well-ordered mind, we will always remember that only our own thoughts cause us unhappiness, not external events beyond our control. Epictetus again:

> Men are disturbed, not by things, but by the principles and notions which they form concerning things.... When therefore we are hindered, or disturbed, or grieved, let us never attribute it to others, but to ourselves; that is, to our own principles.

The disordered mind tortures itself by trying to control that which it cannot. Therefore, Epictetus insists, "Do not seek to have events happen as you want them to, but instead want them to happen as they do happen, and your life will go well."

Golf Drill: Count Your Collapses

Goal setting is essential if we are hoping to progress and improve. Always pick small, realistic goals initially and then move on to larger ones.

One game you can play to help control you mind is very simple. Just count the number of times you became upset during a round. Put a check on your scorecard whenever you're frustrated and tally up the number at the end. Try to reduce that number by one the next time you play and then reduce it one more every time thereafter. By tracking your progress, your goals will become achievable, and pretty soon, you'll teach yourself how to play frustration-free rounds.

The Stoic Golfer

The most powerful person on the planet in his time, the emperor Marcus Aurelius, woke up every morning and told himself that life is far from perfect. The most powerless of people on the planet in his time, the slave Epictetus, told himself the same. We golfers are neither as powerful nor as powerless as they were, so we should have no excuse not to follow their advice.

These are the lessons all golfers must take from the Stoics:

1) Accept the inevitability of frustration.
2) Give up trying to control everything that you can't control.
3) Only control what you can: your mental attitude.

And if you really want to be an invincible Stoic, you should remember to say out loud before every single round, "Today, I will be flustered and frustrated, perturbed and pained, angered and annoyed in every way imaginable; when I am, I will remember that everything happens for a reason. I will keep my cool." This attitude just might be the key to a happy life and a low-scoring round.

9 THE THEOLOGICAL GOLFER

"We have no intention of making the whole golf course 'fair.'"

—David McLay Kidd, Golf Course Architect,
as reported by Scott Gummer
in *The Seventh at St. Andrews*

OH, great Course Architect (CA), hear my lament and answer my prayers: "Why did you put the fairway bunker where I always drive my ball? Why do you tempt me to reach the green in two on a par 5 when I always fall short in the water? Why did you make the entire right side of the fairway on the very first hole out-of-bounds? Why, CA, if you are supposed to be a good CA, do you cause so much suffering? Why did you make the golf course so unfair? Please, dear CA, I humbly beseech you: explain the ways of CA to golfers!"

Such laments are common, not only on the golf course but

throughout human history. Why did God create a universe full of misery and evil? Why does He allow pricks to prosper and saints to suffer? Why is life so unfair?

God would respond no differently than a course architect: He had no intention of making the universe "fair" in the sense that many complaining mortals use the word. After all, "fair" is a concept that humans and golfers misuse all the time. Somehow, it's always "fair" when we get a good (yet undeserved) break, but it's never "fair" when we get a bad break. Our pathetic human memories are woefully short.

Still, it is worth pursuing the question of the inherent fairness and justice of human life. Indeed, one of the greatest challenges for philosophers throughout history has been to prove not only that God exists, but that He is a good, gentle, kind, just and merciful God.

The Dark Ages

The Greek thinkers Plato and Aristotle have shaped pretty much the entire history of Western thought. Even though the Romans conquered the Greeks by force of arms in 146 BC, Greek ideas proved superior to Roman ones. The Romans, impressed by Greek philosophy, spread it throughout the Empire, from Britain in the northwest all the way to Egypt in the southeast. Although the Empire was Roman, its ideas were Greek.

In roughly the 3rd century AD, another intellectual force, which had its roots both in Greek philosophy and Jewish spirituality, arose: Christianity. When Emperor Constantine (c. 272-337 AD) converted to Christianity and made it the official religion of the Roman Empire, he inaugurated the era in which philosophy was dominated by the Catholic Church, an era that lasted about 1,000 years, from 400 to 1400 AD.

This epoch, called variously the Middle Ages, the Medieval Period or the Dark Ages, stands between the order, stability and discipline of the Roman period and the reemergence of secular art and culture in the Renaissance. Except for some brief periods of peace, the Dark Ages were a time of upheaval, war, disease, poverty and illiteracy. The only institution that provided the stability and calm required to pursue philosophy was the Catholic Church, which is why the philosophy of this long period of Western history is dominated by Catholic thinkers.

The first great Christian philosopher was Augustine of Hippo (354-430 AD). Like many of the philosophers we have studied in previous chapters, Augustine was convinced that living a happy life was the purpose of existence. The question was how to achieve that goal. Both Greek thinkers, like Aristotle and Epicurus, and the Roman advocates of Stoicism, like Marcus Aurelius and Epictetus, insisted that happiness could come through managing one's own life. Furthermore, they thought that we did not need a god to live a happy life; we only needed to control ourselves and understand our small role in the universe.

Augustine was different. He insisted that we are incapable of achieving happiness on our own; we need God to complete us. First, however, Augustine had to prove that God exists, and he expended a great deal of effort in an attempt to prove that He does. Proving that God exists was the intellectual fashion that Augustine began, and most medieval thinkers following him took a stab, but they never quite did prove it beyond a reasonable doubt.

St. Thomas Aquinas

Augustine was the leading light of the Middle Age until Thomas Aquinas (1225-1274 AD) appeared on the scene nearly one thousand years later. Aquinas was born close to Naples. He was cut out for the priesthood from the tender age of five, when he was sent to study with the Benedictine monks at Montecassino. From there, he proceeded to study at the University of Naples, then Cologne, and then the University of Paris. His adult life was spent lecturing in Rome and Paris, and he is remembered for producing volumes upon volumes of letters, sermons and books about theology and philosophy.

Aquinas, like Augustine, spent a tremendous amount of time and energy trying to prove the existence of a good God. Rather than looking at their lengthy and complicated proofs, let us assume there is an all-knowing, all-powerful, and perfectly good

God. Once we do, the following important questions arise:

1) Why did God create intelligent agents (humans) who make bad decisions and do evil?

2) Why did a good God even allow for the possibility of evil, suffering, and bad decisions to exist when He created the world?

3) If God wanted us to be good, why did He create luck, which sometimes rewards the bad and punishes the good?

Bad Decisions

On the first question, Aquinas makes the startling point that no one intentionally makes a bad decision nor willingly does evil. He says in the *Summa contra Gentiles*, "Every intelligent agent tends towards something in so far as he considers the object under the rational character of a good.... So, if this object is not good but bad, this will be apart from his intention." This proposition forces us to acknowledge that even people who do evil believe that they are doing good. According to Aquinas, even evil men like Pol Pot and Charles Manson *believe* they are doing the right thing, even though they aren't. In Aquinas' view, God created us in order to be good, but sometimes we make bad decisions that we only realize were bad after the fact (this is the "object" apart from the "intention").

This truth is immediately established on the golf course. How many of us have attempted a trick shot from behind a bush with all the confidence in the world, only to miss completely or strike the ball so poorly that we are in an even worse position than when we started? We *intended* to hit the shot of the century, but we failed miserably. Like God, CA knows that we are trying to play well on the course, but that we often make poor decisions. We always intend to do good, but sometimes we are misguided. As Aquinas insists, "Evil occurs apart from intention." So do bad shots.

Golf Tip: Managing Difficult Shots and Playing It Safe

As Aquinas would argue, we are all trying to do good on the course, although sometimes we unintentionally harm ourselves and do evil. Often, we try to hit that perfect shot or extricate ourselves from a troubled position, but attempting the impossible results in even more serious problems. So a word or two on factors that come into play when attempting difficult shots would be appropriate.

Generally, I would suggest that "playing safe" will be the best option 99 percent of the time when faced with a choice between playing safe and trying to pull off that difficult shot. On the other hand, for most people this is just a game and it should be enjoyed as a game; so what's the harm in giving it a go once in a while?

If you are just playing for fun, you should go for it. But if you are trying to put a round together and you are faced with a difficult shot, there are certain factors to consider.

Firstly, what are your odds of successfully executing this shot? And if you do execute, what are the advantages of doing so? If by forcing a shot over water, you still do not reach the green, you must ask yourself if it was worth the extra anxiety and stress. If the result is advantageous and you are on the green in less than regulation, then it sometimes is worth the risk.

In pro-ams I often see amateurs trying to pull off the miracle one-in-a-hundred shot. I applaud their confidence and positivity; however, the sheer fact that they are attempting a difficult shot that they probably have never practiced tends to lead to the mistakes that will result in failure. Anxiety levels increase when we are attempting something difficult, which in turn leads to tension in the body, which in turn leads to the swing becoming much faster than normal. The resulting swing rarely gets the result that is hoped for, and once again we find ourselves playing from a similar area or sometimes even the exact same one since we "whiffed" the original shot.

I return to a point I made earlier. Club and amateur golfers have handicaps for a reason, but they rarely try to manage their way around the course with their handicap in mind. They always try to play the *course as a tour professional by aiming for par on every hole. If a mistake is made and they find themselves off track, more often than not chipping out to the fairway and accepting the fact that they may drop a shot or two is normally the better option.*

If you do decide to "go for it," try to err on the side of caution. If hitting over water, aim for the shortest carry and hit one more club than you think you need. Concentrate even harder on the fundamentals of the set-up and ensure you focus on the ball. A great rule of thumb is to swing a little slower and watch the ball go longer.

Aquinas reminds us that we often do evil to ourselves unintentionally. A little bit of patience and prudence when managing difficulties on the course will ensure you do not compound that evil.

Free Will

Now that we see that evil occurs as a result of ignorance, not bad intention, we can assess the next question: Why did a good God even allow for the possibility of evil, suffering, and bad decisions to exist when He created the world? Aquinas turned to the idea of free will in order to address this question. God didn't create human beings to act as robots, doing whatever he said. He gave us free will in order that we might choose good over evil and kindness over selfishness. If God did not allow for evil in the universe, many good things could never exist. Aquinas again:

> There would not be the patience of the just if there were not the malice of their persecutors.... If evil were totally excluded from the whole of things by divine providence, a multitude of good things would have to be sacrificed.... Taken away, indeed, would be the praise of human virtue which is nothing, if man does not act freely.

For Aquinas, the freedom to choose good over evil is essential to God's plan.

Free will is an obvious characteristic of the golfing universe as well. We may complain about CA's design, because he tempts us to go for the green in two on a long par 5 with the green protected by water. Or let's say you hit a straight drive that ends up in a nasty bunker that CA deliberately put smack in the middle of the fairway. You could certainly complain and say that a bunker in the middle of the fairway isn't "fair" because it "punishes" a good drive, but CA would argue you needed to consider that fact when you chose to unleash your driver instead of your 3-wood.

No matter what we think, CA's design is just and fair in the ideal and perfect sense of the term. The decisions we freely make allow us to experience highs and lows of a round. We are only able to feel the elation of doing good and the shame of doing evil because we have free will.

Golf History: On Free Will

In the movie Tin Cup, *a scene at the end of the movie shows Roy (Kevin Costner's character) hitting a shot into the water hazard again and again and again. He refuses to give up and, in doing so, exudes Aquinas' concept of free will.*

This scene is based on an actual event that happened to Gary McCord, the commentator with the handlebar mustache in the movie, who is an actual commentator and a retired pro golfer. In a 1987 tournament he had a shot similar to Roy's. He needed a birdie to win and went for it. Splash! Instead of moving the ball forward as the rules allowed, he insisted on playing the same shot from the same spot. He hit the water over and over again until he finally made the shot, but the debacle cost him fifteen strokes. This is a fine example of a golfer being a little bit too profligate with his precious gift of free will.

Luck

We have seen that both evil and free will must exist in order for the perfect universe to function. Still, evil and free will don't explain why luck exists. Aquinas argued that God wants us to freely choose to be good because being good should lead to reward and being evil should lead to punishment. However, our experience shows us quite the opposite. History is littered with the corpses of countless saints who were crucified, fed to lions, burned at the stake or drawn-and-quartered by rich and powerful tyrants.

So if God really wanted us to freely choose to be good because that's the way to guarantee success, why did he create luck, which more often than not seems to punish the good? The answer to this question requires that we reconsider free will. If God has planned for absolutely everything, then everything would happen according to a pre-determined plan, *by necessity*, not because people make free choices. In other words, if luck did not exist, free will could not either. Aquinas argues, "If some things did not occur in rare instances, all things would happen by necessity.... But it would be contrary to the essential character of divine providence if all things occurred by necessity." If there were no luck, there would be no free will either. The two go hand-in-hand.

To illustrate this point further, think about golf. If you were always to fail or succeed based on the quality of the shot you played, the game would lose its appeal. How many times have you hit a good shot and been punished? And how many times have you skulled or shanked the ball and ended up with a miraculous birdie chance? Aquinas would remind us that even though we *usually* get what we deserve, luck is a necessary component of life.

CA also knew that not everyone would go for the pin in two on a long par 5 with the green surrounded by water. Of course, our friend who can't ever make it over the water might hit a miracle shot that skips across the water four times before crawling up to the green. Why is he rewarded for that bad decision? Well, CA doesn't give breaks to the jerks who don't deserve it nor does he punish those who do the right thing—luck, not CA, is responsible.

Golf History: The Bad-Luck Shark

Luck is evident throughout the game of golf, but I don't think luck is something a player should dwell on. Taken as a whole, golf is a game of skill, mental strength and character, not a game of chance. Mastering the technical aspects of golf is much more critical to success than getting lucky. With a better understanding of how the swing mechanics work, it is possible to rectify mistakes with the swing when out on the course, and not just hope for a lucky break.

Saying that, there have been many examples of "bad luck" throughout the game. An uncanny amount of this misfortune has happened to the Australian Greg Norman. During the 1986 PGA Championships played at Inverness Golf Club, Norman was leading but carded a 76 for the final round which, of course, could have ruined any chance he had of winning the title. However, and not for the first time, it was Bob Tway's unbelievable (lucky?) chip in on the 72nd hole that allowed him to eventually win by two shots.

In 1987 Norman was tied for the lead after the last round of the Masters after shooting a final round 72. This meant a playoff ensued between Norman, Larry Mize and the Spaniard Severiano Ballesteros. After Ballesteros was eliminated, Norman and Mize were left to fight it out. Mize missed the green to the right and faced an extremely difficult chip shot from some 45 yards away, whilst Norman hit a fine approach onto the green, giving himself a possible birdie chance. What followed was as miraculous as it was unbelievable—was it luck? From a seemingly impossible position, Mize holed his shot whilst Norman left his putt short of the hole. Norman would once again miss his chance to don the green jacket at the 1989 Masters. On the 72nd hole, he needed a birdie to win or a par to make the playoff, but he bogeyed instead after apparently hitting the wrong club off the tee! Bad luck?

Later that same year during the Open Championship at Royal Troon, he carded an outstanding final round 64, which got him into a playoff with Mark Calcavecchia and Wayne Grady. The fourth hole of the playoff saw Norman and Calcavecchia on level pegging, but Calcavecchia sliced his shot to the right, leaving the door open wide enough for Norman to stride through. Norman decided on a three wood to avoid the bunkering down the fairway; unfortunately, his ball took a bad (unlucky?) bounce off a down slope, and to his amazement *it found the fairway bunker some 310 yards away.*

Calcavecchia proceeded to play a fabulous (lucky?) approach shot to five feet from the hole, forcing Norman to try and match Calcavecchia's shot from a much more difficult predicament. Norman fired into the ball, which caught the lip and ran into a second bunker—more bad luck?

As if this wasn't bad enough, whilst Norman was beavering away at trying salvage par, Peter Alliss, who was commentating for BBC TV, had his comments and predictions heard throughout the course due to a short circuit with the electrical cables, thus allowing not only the TV audience to hear, but also everyone else on the course, including Norman himself! Norman unfortunately thinned his subsequent shot out of bounds and the Open title went to Mark Calcavecchia.

The Masters once again came to haunt Norman, this time in 1996 when playing with Nick Faldo in the final pairing. Norman was protecting a six-shot lead, but ended up losing it anyway. It is widely regarded that this time Faldo won the Masters because of some superb last-day golf rather than because Norman collapsed or was the victim of bad luck.

So, it would be naive to say that luck does not play its part in golf; after all, every chip-in or "hole-in-one" has some element of luck to it. But try not to curse your opponent's next good break, and instead expect the odd good break yourself as much as you are prepared to manage your next bout of misfortune.

The Perfect Universe

St. Thomas Aquinas has shown us that the universe is perfect, even when it appears to be flawed. He says the world is fair, even when it appears to be unfair. God is perfect—perfectly good, perfectly just, perfectly kind, and perfectly fair—so the universe that He created must be perfect too. The evils that exist only appear to be evil to human brains that cannot understand why evil *must* exist—so free will can exist as well. The existence of luck or chance is similarly necessary for the perfect world—chance makes free will possible.

The evils that we want to blame God for are evils of our own choosing. The bad decisions we want to blame on CA are also freely chosen. If we heap misery on ourselves and others, it is not because God wanted us to be evil. Sadly, our righteous intent often does not guarantee a successful outcome—*hence, the existence of sins and bad shots*. But by giving us the gift of freewill, God gave us the choice to be good. Without that free choice, neither the universe nor golf could exist.

The Perfection of the Golfing Universe

A curious idea of the universe exists in many golfers' brains.

Amateurs are susceptible to it, but pros are as well. It is a false idea. It is a self-destructive idea. It is an irrational idea. It is an immature idea. What is it? It is the refusal to accept the perfection of the golfing universe, just as many of us refuse to accept the perfection of the actual universe.

Golf is perfect in the same way life is, but many people don't comprehend this. On 20 June 2010, Teddy Greenstein of the *LA Times* reported on Ryan Moore and Graham McDowell's reactions to the set-up of the course for the 2010 US Open at Pebble Beach, a tournament that was won by McDowell, curiously enough, with even par.

Moore complained that the course, in general, "doesn't reward good golf shots like Augusta does." He continued, "I don't understand why you'd have a tournament that doesn't reward good golf shots."

He singled out both the 14th hole and the 17th hole, a tricky par 3, for particular criticism. Of the 17th he said, "It would take not much to make that green at least halfway reasonable, and they refuse to do it. I don't know what they're trying to demand," Moore grumbled. "If you can't even hit a shot that can stay on the green, where's the skill involved? I just don't understand." He concluded, "I think they go for a spectacle; they want some hole to draw attention and make everybody look stupid, I guess."

Interestingly enough, the winner of the tournament, Graham McDowell, called 17 "one of the greatest holes in world golf," although he added that it was "borderline unfair," which I interpret to mean "extremely difficult."

Moore's flawed line of reasoning is similar to all of the complaints that the universe is not perfect or that life is unfair. Let's identify the flaws of the argument as Aquinas would (without being unduly harsh on Mr. Moore):

(1) Obviously, there is no positive outcome that can be derived from complaint because complaining will not change the natural laws of the world for you. In this respect, all golfers and all creatures are subject to the same rules. The physics of ball striking and the laws of gravity apply to both Moore and McDowell, to both you and me. This is the purest form of equality and fairness that both God and golf provide. If the 14th hole or the 17th hole, or if life itself is difficult, it presents the same difficulties to all alike.

(2) Another argument has to do specifically with equality. Everyone had to play the 14th hole four times. For the whole championship, McDowell played the hole +1. Grégory Havret, who came in second place 1 stroke back, played it even par. Els, who came in third 2 strokes back, played it +2. Moore, who finished tied for 33rd, 12 strokes back, played it +1, just like the winner McDowell!

Regarding the 17th, McDowell played it +3 over the course of the championship, and Moore played it +2! In other words, Moore played the "unfair" holes 1 stroke better than McDowell, but he still lost.

Not only did everyone have to play 14 and 17 four times, but they had to play the whole course four times as well. This is the very definition of fairness. Now, one might complain that the conditions might change over the course of the day, which gives some players an advantage over others. If we just take one tournament into account, a player could be unlucky because he is forced to play in worse conditions than everyone else. However, in one tournament he will have luck and get the benefit of good conditions. Therefore, even the course conditions do not indicate any degree of intrinsic unfairness.

(3) Moore claimed that the USGA did not even do the minimum to make the green "half-way reasonable." Reason has nothing to do with golf given points (1) and (2). Indeed, we might also complain to God and say that he did not even make living a happy life half-way reasonable. Aquinas would beg to differ. He would say that the world is perfectly reasonable; however, we often fail to recognize its reasonableness. We make ourselves the cause of our own anguish at the presumed unfairness of the world. Still, everyone has free will. If we think the world is so very unreasonable, we can always end our lives. Moore, too, did not have to continue playing.

The Cardinal Virtues

Aquinas would not appreciate complaints about the perfection of the world. Indeed, if he were to advise a golfer on the appropriate attitude toward being successful at golf, he would discuss the cardinal virtues of temperance, courage, justice and prudence. Aquinas would argue that the winner of a golf tournament will be the player who exhibits these qualities more than others. The winner inevitably exhibits these virtues better than anyone else. The winner at the game of life will exhibit these same traits as well. The losers, in both golf and life, will not have mastered these virtues and probably will have developed some vices along the way.

It is important to note that, like Aristotle, Aquinas believed that we must not simply claim we have these virtues. We must habitually practice them in order to have them. Similarly, when we act in ways that are not successful, we develop vices.

Temperance

Let's look at temperance first. Aquinas suggests that we have both rational and animalistic thoughts. Since we have a body that is affected by pleasure, we often act in such a way to increase our physical pleasure and reduce our pain. When we only seek physical pleasure, however, we develop the vice of gluttony. What we need, then, is a virtue to keep our physical desires in check. This is temperance, which allows a successful golfer to abstain from staying up all night and drinking during a tournament. Most golfers have developed the virtue of temperance throughout their lives. The long hours of practice and training that they put in are not necessarily pleasurable. However, they recognize that hard work is important to succeeding, so they abstain from physical urges.

Golf Tip: The Temperate Golfer

The attitude towards physical health has changed amongst touring professionals over the last ten to fifteen years and some of this has to be attributed to the likes of Tiger Woods, who amplified the need for other players to embark on both a healthier diet and a more rigorous physical training regime. Before Tiger, the usual after-round activities were more "bar"-based, and visits to the gym and personal trainers were few and far between.

Tiger and the new breed of tour pros exude temperance. Speaking from experience, during the Open Championships Tiger will go to the gym early in the morning prior to going to the course. He will eat healthy, energy-packed snacks and drink plenty of water to remain hydrated during a round. He will once again go to the gym later that day and eat well in the evening. This is a busy day's work, and I am sure that he does not look forward to the early rise to go to the gym, but he realizes the importance of the strict regime and staying true to the cause whilst resisting the easier sometimes more pleasant alternatives.

If you do have ambitions to become a tour professional, then there really is no choice—you have to embark on a strict regime and a healthy lifestyle. Eating well and visiting the gym five or six times a week must become a natural part of your life. Employing personal trainers who can prepare golf-specific exercise routines for you is a must, and staying committed to this regimented way of life is essential. However, even recreational club golfers can become temperate golfers by deciding to practice a little more in order to improve the weaker aspects of their game.

Even a small commitment to temperance would be helpful. Decide to arrive at the course 30 minutes earlier than normal each time you play, so you can at least stretch, do a proper warm up and hit practice balls.

Courage

Having courage means possessing the ability to be courageous in the face of challenges both great and small. There will always be challenges in our lives. We could blame God for putting them there, but that would be irrational. Challenges exist so we may overcome them, and we develop the virtue of courage so that we may stay focused on our goals even when circumstances go against us. Aquinas would suggest that we all should focus on developing our courage.

Golf Tip: The Courageous Golfer

We face the question of fortitude many times during a round of golf. Questions about our strength of mind and character, our endurance and resilience, are continually being asked as we make our way from the first tee to the eighteenth hole.

One of the many tips that I have received and never forgotten is this: when we are having a bad day and the ball seems to want to stay to the side of the course and hide within the trees, treat each shot as a challenge. Try not complaining about the lie and the difficult shot you are now faced with, but instead treat it as a day of challenges. Just how well can you play a shot as difficult as this? Just how good a score can we still achieve on a day like today? Treat every shot as a new challenge. Stay strong and courageous and don't let the bad breaks dampen your fortitude.

Here's a story about battling against the odds and staying strong when the chips are down.

Justin Rose was a prolific amateur golfer winning many of the top prizes in amateur golf. The culmination of this amateur career would have to be playing in the 1998 British Open as the youngest amateur ever to qualify. Justin had a wonderful week and miraculously finished 4th. He decided to turn pro the next week and because of his placing at the Open, he was given many invites to forthcoming events. He then subsequently missed the next twenty-one cuts!

Many "experts" were telling Justin that he had turned pro too early, that he wasn't ready, and that his swing was not yet mature enough to survive the tour. But he stuck to his beliefs and his swing mechanics, initially taught to him by his father Ken, and showed much fortitude and courage to fight through the bad times and come out the other side a stronger player.

Just when things were looking up on the golf front, Rose learned that his father had been diagnosed with cancer.

Rose struggled to cope in the wake of his father's death, but it was not too long before his talent was shining through once more. Justin has gone on to be a world class golfer challenging for the top spot on numerous occasions. He earned over $3,000,000 in 2011 and won the U.S. Open at Merion in 2013.

This kind of strength of character is vital if you are going to not only compete at the highest level as Justin has, but also be able to fight the endless fights we face on the golf course on a day-to-day basis.

Justice

The third cardinal virtue is justice. Justice is a curious virtue because it has to do primarily with how we understand others. Justice forces us to recognize that everyone is deserving of the same rights and treatment that we deserve.

Golf, with its emphasis on sportsmanship, rules, and fairness, ranks this virtue more highly than any other. Curiously, Aquinas says that justice involves realizing that we are not special. We are no more deserving of good treatment than others. We are no more deserving of reward or punishment than anyone else. Complaints about a course being too hard would be the most problematic for Aquinas. A mature sense of justice would require that we acknowledge that everyone in a tournament is in the same boat. While we might wish that life or a golf course rewarded us as we think we deserve, a mature sense of justice at the same time reminds us to acknowledge that fundamental equality is a good thing, which we ought not to complain about. The winners get what they deserve, and the losers do as well. The appropriate response to a competitor who beats you is not to suggest that the course was unfair or that it was a lucky win. To say the course or luck determined the match is to also imply that your competitor won unfairly—because of luck or chance but not because of skill, effort, or hard work. Such an attitude towards an opponent illustrates an underdeveloped sense of justice.

Golf Tip: The Just Golfer

At the 1999 Open Championship at Carnoustie, many of the players complained about the difficulty of the course, primarily the length of the rough. They renamed the course "Car-nasty." However, complaining about the course was futile. The rough was the same for everyone; the course was the same for everyone.

Ironically, each and every week on tour there is a case of injustice. Depending on what side of the draw you are on, you may be unlucky enough to catch the worst of the weather both the day you tee off in the morning and then the following day when your tee-time flips to the afternoon. There may be some "woe-is-me" in the changing rooms after the round, but it is generally accepted that sometimes you are just going to get unlucky with the tee times and the weather.

Also, if you are going to play 18 holes and expect 100 percent justice for the actions and shots you are making, you may be expecting a little too much and gearing yourself up for quite a fall. Unfortunately, this game is not an exact science, and therefore there will be many times out there that you really did deserve much more than you got. But as you see your perfect tee shot hit the sprinkler head and ricochet into the woods, remember justice is not a part of this game as much as we would all like it to be.

During a round of golf, there are plenty of opportunities to behave as Aquinas would have us do. We are not special, and everyone does deserve the same treatment, so the next time we are on the tee, make a determined effort to watch the tee shots of your playing partners instead of putting your club back or chatting and maybe missing their shots completely.

If looking for a potentially lost ball, look with vigor and enthusiasm just as you would wish your playing partners to do for you. We all have bad days.

One other point: I often see mid- to low-handicappers getting very impatient with beginner golfers either in their group or up ahead. Although it is just as important that the beginner understands the etiquette of the game and the courtesy of letting people play through, try to remember we were all beginners at one time, and they are probably even more frustrated than you are. Help them, if possible, and allow them the patience and courtesy that you would like to have shown to yourself.

Prudence

Aquinas' final cardinal virtue is prudence, which is the virtue that we remember Epicurus prized above all others. Prudence is an intellectual virtue and might also be considered wisdom. The wise golfer knows his strengths and weaknesses. He knows how to approach every course, every round and every shot to maximize his chances for success. Clearly, a golfer who wins a major tournament makes more correct decisions than his opponents. One could also argue that he makes the fewest mistakes. Successful golfers, through playing a round or tournament, maximize their chances for success by making the best decisions that give them the best chance for victory. They give themselves the best possible chance to win.

Golf Tip: The Prudent Golfer

Prudence is vital if we are going to be successful. As Aquinas might argue, a prudent golfer is one who not only makes fewer mistakes than his or her opponents, but also makes better decisions throughout the round. This can include when to play safe and when to be a little more aggressive. Prudence for a golfer can also be thought of as being a better thinker on the course or being better at course management. Playing to your strengths will not only keep you grounded and relaxed, but will also allow you to fulfill your potential on the course without the normal distractions that plague one or two holes of the round.

Being prudent on the course does not just happen, it is something that needs to be practiced and honed. I think it would be prudent of you, the next time you play, to make a plan for the round. Decide prior to the round, first, how many pars you realistically think you can make and, second, how many bogeys your handicap allows you to make and on which holes. When in trouble, chip out, not just the one time, but every time for the round. Then analyze your round later. You may be surprised by how well you played—because you were prudent and didn't waste strokes.

Conclusion

Perhaps we are in a better position now to understand why both God and the Course Architect decided not to make the universe or the golf course "fair," why they decided to allow evil and suffering in the world, why they elected to give us the gift of free will, why they created luck (which sometimes punishes good people and rewards evil ones), and why both the universe and the game of golf are, in fact, perfect. If the design were any different, we imperfect humans could never experience the highs and lows of life or a round of golf. We could not choose our own actions or our own shots. We could not choose to do good or evil to ourselves or others. We could neither be rewarded not punished by a lucky or unlucky break. Such a game is not the game of golf, which is a game that is loved for the same reason people love life.

The universe is perfect, but we are not. However, we can

strive for perfection by cultivating the cardinal virtues. It is, of course, no coincidence that all winners of major championships exhibit the virtues of temperance, fortitude, justice and prudence more than the rest of the field. And to the losers who complain about the difficulty of the course or the role that luck plays in the game, ask them to present a champion who does not exhibit all of these virtues in abundance.

For Aquinas, being good meant striving to be as close to absolute goodness (God) as possible. The happiest people are those who strive to be good. So, too, the best golfers are those who understand the perfection that the Course Architect intends. In this respect, the winner of a golfing competition is like the winner in life. He or she comes closest to achieving perfection on the course.

Sadly, no one will ever achieve perfection on the course, nor will we live the perfect lives that Aquinas' kind and gentle God intends us to live. Exactly how far are we, poor hackers, from perfection? The perfect round is eighteen strokes, eighteen holes-in-one.

CONCLUSION: FROM ANCIENT TO MODERN PHILOSOPHY

WE have seen that ancient Greek and Roman philosophers had a number of intellectual interests. These provide a basis for understanding the dominant themes of both ancient and medieval thought as well as modern thought; these themes are *metaphysics*, *happiness*, *epistemology*, and *teleology*.

The pre-Socratics, such as Heraclitus and Parmenides, were concerned with comprehending the fundamental nature of the universe, the first major theme. The ancient term for this pursuit is *metaphysics* (although modern philosophers would define the term differently). Heraclitus insisted that the world was constantly changing, that the only truth is that everything is in constant flux. Parmenides insisted that, even though our senses reveal constant change, our senses deceive us. Everything, he argues, stays the same. So, is change all that is real, or does everything stay the same? Approaching golf from the perspective of change or stasis yields important insights. In some respects, even the same golf course is always different due to changing course conditions. Managing those conditions is critical. At the same time, approaching each shot on any course with the same routine helps us to develop the confidence we need to succeed.

These disputes about metaphysics seemed too abstract for the Sophists such as Protagoras, who believed instead that philosophers ought to focus their energy on teaching people how to live successfully in a world in which practical skills and knowledge are more important than idle philosophical disputes. Learning how to be a powerful member of society, they suggested, would lead to *happiness*, our second theme. Sophists believed that truth was relative to the individual. No one is right or wrong. No one has the truth. The truth doesn't exist. They would suggest that a happy golfer is one who believes in his own truth, his own style, his own swing, no matter what the experts say.

Achieving happiness was also a primary focus of Plato's philosophy, although he needed to prove that there was such a thing as truth in order to do so. The study of knowledge itself is our third theme. The technical term for this is *epistemology*. How can we know knowledge is even possible? How do we determine what is true and false? What is a more reliable path for finding truth: reason or sense perception?

Plato needed to prove that knowledge was possible for a number of reasons. First, he needed to show that the Sophists were wrong when they insisted that the truth was relative. If the truth is only what each of us believes—if a steak is neither tasty nor gross; if the earth is neither flat nor round; if tyranny is neither good nor bad—then there could be no way to improve Athenian government and society. Plato, however, showed decisively that there is such a thing as objective truth. Following the truth would then lead to a better government, a better society, and happier people. Crucially for golfers, he also shows us that there really is an objective basis for improving one's golf.

Plato's student Aristotle was also concerned with happiness. However, he also was concerned with figuring out why stuff happens. He was interested in causes and final purposes. The study of final purposes is called *teleology*. If we can discover why things exist or what their purpose is, then we can figure out how we should live as well. Aristotle insisted that everything has a purpose, which is to achieve its own *telos*, its own full development. The *telos* of a human being is to live a good, happy, well-rounded, comfortable life. Once we know that this is our purpose, we have a target to aim at, and we can then set about fulfilling that task. Golfers, once they have a clear conception of their target, have a better chance of hitting it.

The other philosophers of ancient Greece and Rome were wholly concerned with discovering the best way to live a happy life. Cynics like Diogenes insisted that the path to happiness required the renunciation of all the luxuries of civilized life, including possessions as well as the desire for power, wealth and social status. Diogenes wants us to quit golf. Hedonists, far from recommending that we forego the luxuries of civilized life, argued that we should participate in as many pleasurable activities as possible. They encourage us to golf as much as possible.

The Epicureans take a mid-point between Cynics and hedonists. They acknowledge that we ought to pursue pleasure, but we should do so in moderation. Furthermore, Epicurus reminds us that there are some pains that we cannot escape, such as physical pain. We ought to train ourselves to endure them. However, he also reminds us that we often cause ourselves mental anguish by being vain and having unrealistic expectations. Failure to meet social expectations may cause us pain; therefore, we ought to be wary of coveting society's approval. Certain pleasures, however, are open to all, regardless of power, wealth and status. Friendship, Epicurus insists, is the greatest happiness. He would suggest that golfing—in moderation and with friends—is a wonderful way to live.

The Stoics were also interested in achieving happiness. Epictetus and Marcus Aurelius took elements of Cynicism and Epicureanism to the extreme in developing the revolutionary philosophy of Stoicism. The way to achieve happiness is to regulate one's own mind. Pain comes from thinking that we have control over things that we really have no control over. Trying to control things out of our control makes us miserable. If we can train ourselves to accept this fact, we will necessarily leave peaceful and contented lives. The Stoics tell us to golf in a state of total mental calm. Bad breaks happen to everyone. When they happen to you, don't think you are somehow being treated badly by the universe. Take the good and the bad the exact same way, and you will be a more successful person and a better golfer.

Following the conversion of the Romans to Christianity, Christian thought became systematized and developed, but Christian thinkers were still heavily influenced by the ancient philosophical themes. Christian philosophy culminated in the works of St. Thomas Aquinas in the 13th century. Aquinas insisted that the origin of all things is an all good, all-powerful, and all-knowing God. Although many golfers assume that the universe is not fair, Aquinas showed us that it is. God gave us free will in order for goodness to exist, and the purpose of a human being is to become closer to God by trying to be as good as possible. Cultivating the cardinal virtues of temperance, fortitude, justice and prudence was the best way to achieve this. These same virtues, we saw, are also crucial for champion golfers.

Aquinas was the last great Catholic thinker of the Middle Ages. Throughout the 1,000-year-long Middle Ages, the Catholic Church was the dominant intellectual force in Western European society. The Church controlled schools and universities, influenced kings and emperors, and dominated social and political life. If you wanted to learn to read and write, you had to go to an institution run by monks or priests and supervised by bishops and the Pope. Organized in a strict hierarchy, the Catholic Church wielded its power through controlling the education system; through conducting sacramental rights, such as baptism and confession, which would guarantee salvation; through granting indulgences, which meant that your sins could be pardoned for a hefty price; and also through threatening people with excommunication, an act that would cast sinners into the never-ending torment of hell.

However, two developments—one in science and the other in religion—began to undermine the Church's near total control over thought.

First, scientific advances served to undermine the power of the Church. Astronomers and mathematicians such as Copernicus, Kepler and Galileo showed that the Sun, not the Earth, was the center of the universe. This heliocentric view undermined two orthodox beliefs—that humans residing upon Earth were the highest forms of God's creation and that God created everything in the universe *for* human beings. The Church staunchly supported the idea that the Earth is the center of the universe; scientific evidence that contradicted this doctrine would necessarily shake the very foundation of the Church's authority. People started asking uncomfortable questions: If the leaders of the Church were wrong about the Earth being the center of the universe, then what else could they be wrong about? If humans are not the center of the universe, if we are just a part of a bigger, indifferent universe, then what is God's relationship to us? Are we the summit of creation or just a cosmic afterthought? Should the truths of religious doctrine be replaced by the truths of science?

Second, the Catholic monk Martin Luther (1483-1546) attacked the Church from a religious perspective (although he along with the Church disagreed with Copernicus' view of a heliocentric universe). Luther began to criticize the corrupt practices of priests, particularly the institution of indulgences. Luther's critiques eventually led to his excommunication. His actions also precipitated innumerable savage wars between those who had rejected the Church's authority and those who remained Catholic. The social order was overturned. Europe was in flames.

It was in this atmosphere of doubt—doubt about the nature of scientific truths and doubt about the Church's claim to absolute truth—that Rene Descartes embarked upon his effort to establish a new way, a new method, to decisively discover the truth. His method—the Cartesian method—represents the birth of modern philosophy.

With Descartes' revolution in thought, Volume II of *The Philosophical Golfer* begins.

ABOUT THE AUTHORS

Dr. Andrew Sola received his Ph.D. from the University of East Anglia in 2003. For over a decade, he has taught philosophy and English at universities around the world, including UMUC in Germany and Italy, Loyola University in Chicago, and UEA in England. His scholarly writing has appeared in the *Literary Encyclopedia*, *Studies in Language and Capitalism*, and the *Journal of Military Ethics*.

PGA golf professional Bruce Loome has taught golf for over 20 years in England, Germany, Portugal, and the United States of America. A British Class A PGA professional, Bruce has also played professionally on the PGA Euro Pro Tour, the Alps Tour, the EPD Tour in Germany, as well as the Belgium PGA Tour. Bruce has worked for Tiger Woods as a personal marshal for the past 14 years and is still employed by him today. He is currently working as a PGA coach at the Oxford Golf Academy in Oxford, England, and is also attached to Studley Wood Golf Club as a playing professional.